HONOUR AND SHAME

To my dearest Zaid and Sara
and in loving memory of my mother

HONOUR AND SHAME
Women in Modern Iraq

Sana al-Khayyat

Saqi Books

British Library Cataloguing in Publication Data
Khayyat, Sana al-
    Honour and shame : women in modern Iraq
    1. Iraq. Women. Social conditions
    I. Title
    305.4209567

    ISBN 0-86356-094-6
    ISBN 0-86356-050-4 pbk

First published 1990 by
Saqi Books, 26 Westbourne Grove
London W2 5RH

© Saqi Books 1990

Typeset by AKM Associates (UK) Ltd, Southall, London
Printed and bound in Great Britain
at The Camelot Press, Trowbridge, Wiltshire.

Contents

Acknowledgements

I wish to thank Elizabeth Hand for reading most of the book and for her advice, support and encouragement. My thanks also go to others such as Ursula Sharma who was my supervisor for the thesis on which the book is based, and to Pat Ager and Maureen Winn for their help and encouragement.

My research would not have been possible without the generous and friendly participation of the women I interviewed and I shall always remain in their debt.

Last but not least, my thanks go to my family, my brothers and sisters, particularly Issam and Farkad who supported me in every possible way. I also thank my children Sara and Zaid for helping me in their own way.

Introduction

This book addresses the experience of Iraqi women: in particular, the process of socialization of female members of the family, female roles and the way women perceive themselves in relation to men and others within the family. It also examines such topics as preparations for marriage, husband-wife relationships, personal interaction between men and women, and the way women are controlled by society through both sexes.

It is written from what might be called a double perspective: Iraqi society is viewed both from the outside and from within. As a sociologist I am trained to be a detached, objective observer. As an Iraqi woman myself, however, I have shared and experienced all the problems of the women of my country, problems that result from their oppression by the patriarchal system in which they live. This oppression is practised upon women by both sexes. In fact, women probably feel a greater direct oppression by members of their own sex than by men, as women practise social control by adopting male ways of thinking and male roles in policing each other. This is particularly true of mothers, mothers-in-law, older women within the family and teachers. Other women such as neighbours play a similar, though often indirect, controlling role through gossip.

The basis for my work was a series of in-depth interviews with Iraqi women, together with the available literature and my own experience and observations as a member of Iraqi society. Since I only interviewed women, it might be objected that my observations on men, their thoughts and attitudes, are one-sided. In Iraq, however, it is highly improbable that a man would answer a researcher's questions directly, especially if the researcher was a woman investigating the position of women in society. Moreover Iraqi men tend to be dismissive of female opinions and to consider women's studies irrelevant.

The following incident illustrates the point. A male friend of my family who is considered well-educated asked me during my fieldwork:

> Why are you wasting time with those stupid women? What can they tell you? Women in general are trouble-makers and unfaithful, and above all they're never satisfied. Take my advice, forget about interviewing them, they can say nothing useful for your research. If you insist on adopting this method, select a few educated men and interview them; they would tell you all you need to know about women.

I believe this opinion to be typical of most Iraqi men.

It is worth pointing out that although my research concentrated on Iraqi women in an urban context, they have much in common with other Arab women in cities throughout the Arab world. Conversely, most of the research on women in other countries that I have quoted here for comparative purposes is equally applicable to Iraqi women.

Since the appearance of Islam in the seventh century and up to the First World War, the Arab world could be considered as one. The majority of its people professed the same faith (Islam), spoke the same language (Arabic) and shared the same culture. There were many influences at work within this vast area, however. Of these, one of particular relevance to my study was the bedouin influence, which has mainly been felt in the eastern part of the Arab world of which Iraq is a part.

My contention is that Iraq is a patriarchal society and that the patriarchal system has been reinforced by bedouin tribal values which have dominated society for a very long time. According to al-Wardi,[1] the Iraqi mentality and social mores during the four centuries of Ottoman rule up to the First World War were closer to those of the bedouin tribe than to those of a centrally organized state. This influence was to have long-term effects: a large majority of the Iraqi population still have a strong belief in *asabiyya* (family spirit). Urban-dwellers also maintain this tradition: a boy from the city 'will feel *asabiyya* in relation to his district instead of to his tribe'.[2] Berger[3] notes that in bedouin society the family and tribe take responsibility for the conduct of their individual members. This is of relevance when we consider the notion of honour and shame–a woman's conduct is not assessed at the individual level; it reflects on the entire family group.

The system of male domination in Iraqi society uses not only bedouin social values but also Islamic ideology as tools to control women. The Quran says:

Men are the protectors and maintainers of women, because god has given the one more strength than the other, and because they support them (*al-Nisa 34*).

This verse (which itself is open to different interpretations) is memorized by schoolchildren throughout the Arab world and is widely quoted by those who see Islam as an oppressive religion. With the growing strength of the Islamic movement in the region, such quotes from the Quran are increasingly

11

resorted to as a justification for women's oppression and low status.

Some writers, including several in the feminist movement, argue that it is not so much the religion which is oppressive but the way in which it has been interpreted in Muslim societies.

The Interviews

All the interviews were held in Baghdad in spring and summer 1982 (during the war with Iran) at venues ranging from schools, illiteracy eradication centres,[4] offices and colleges to people's homes. In all, I interviewed fifty women, asking them a series of detailed questions about their childhood, adolescence and marital life. Only married women were included; in Iraq it is extremely unusual for a woman to remain single and answers from unmarried women would not have been representative. I divided the women into three categories, according to their educational level. The first category consisted of illiterate housewives attending an illiteracy eradication centre. The second comprised teachers at two Baghdad schools. The third category was that of 'higher professionals'–heads of departments running ministries, lawyers, lecturers, and so on. It should be noted that these were all urban women–research among rural and peasant women would have revealed different life-styles, although I believe the same general pattern of oppression prevails.

Housewives

There were sixteen housewives, representing working-class and lower middle-class women and ranging in age from 20 to 49. Economically dependent, most had married very young. Their male relatives had made all decisions concerning their lives: their fathers and brothers made such decisions for them before marriage, and after marriage their husbands would take over the role of decision-maker, subsequently passing it to their sons.

When illiteracy eradication was made compulsory in Iraq in 1978 and all those who were illiterate were obliged by law to attend classes, women enjoyed this opportunity to mix with other people and to leave their home freely to go to school. It was almost as a by-product that they learned to read and write.

The majority of these housewives' fathers were polygamous. The women's own marriages were entirely arranged by their families and many had not been consulted beforehand; they married mainly to please their parents. They also believed that marriage would solve many of their problems and relieve the parental pressures on them. No matter what kind of life these women were living with their husband, it was out of the question for them to divorce him–their family would only take the woman back if it was the husband who divorced her. Despite the pain caused to a wife by the prospect of her husband engaging in a second marriage, many women accepted it. One even helped her husband find a second wife in order to prevent him divorcing her. While a woman in this category will feel much stronger and more secure after the birth of her first son, the birth of a daughter brings her less status.

These women suffered from many personal and social problems. Perhaps the worst was alcoholism among their husbands. Many said their husband was very irritable and persistently shouted at them and the children. Although they admitted their sufferings, they nevertheless seemed to accept life as it was, sacrificing their lives to the family and thinking they were not important. Overwhelmingly, they perceived themselves as housewives and mothers. A good man, in their opinion, was one who comes home with a bag of fruit or something for the children and who does not drink alcohol, shout at them or beat the children. They had very few other ambitions, living their life vicariously through their children.

13

Teachers

The second group was composed of twenty teachers aged between 21 and 54. They were representative of the lower-middle and upper-middle classes, though some came from working-class families. Most middle-class women in Iraq are educated to at least primary-school level, particularly those under the age of 50. Most of the women in this group had a BA; the rest had taken a teaching certificate after high school.

Although in general the teachers were educated, enterprising and public-spirited, their marital life differed little from that of the illiterate housewives. Although they worked, they did not see themselves as the family breadwinner. They had fewer children than the housewives (ranging between one and four, though one woman had six). Their standard of living depended mainly on the husband's financial situation. Most of them lived in relatively good conditions, coming from socially mobile classes and educated families.

Many complained of the all-female environment at work, saying they preferred to work with men in a mixed situation. They held stereotyped views of the sexes, believing that men are 'more educated', 'more flexible' and 'emotionally stronger and kinder' than women. Women, on the other hand, were said to be 'stupid', to 'concern themselves with trivial matters', to have 'unstable personalities', to be 'led by their emotions' and to be 'unable to play a leading role in society'.

Higher Professionals

The majority of the fourteen women in higher positions came from the middle classes. Some were university lecturers, one was the head of department at a ministry, one was a lawyer and another was engaged as a researcher. Ten held a BA, two had an MA and the remaining two had a high school diploma. Their husbands had all received a higher education and most held relatively good posts, though not necessarily higher than those of their wives.

The women in this group (who were aged between 26 and 58) were a little more self-confident and independent than those in the other two categories. Some were nevertheless leading very unhappy married lives, though most tried to avoid answering some of my questions concerning their personal relationship with their husbands, particularly sexual relations.

Similar to the teachers, most of these women preferred a mixed working environment rather than working with other women only. They also preferred to have a male boss. They tended to have fewer children than the other two categories, due to their busy lives: most had between one and three, apart from two who had four and five respectively. Many of their problems related to the complexity of their jobs, which took up most of the daylight hours. Their standard of living was high and they were all earning very high salaries,[5] as were their husbands.

Ethnic and Religious Background
No attempt was made to classify the women according to religion or ethnic group. It should be noted, however, that although Iraqis are predominantly Muslim Arabs and speak Arabic, my interviewees included four Kurdish women. Comprising some 20% of the population and living mainly in the north of the country, the Kurds are one of the largest ethnic minorities in Iraq. Being non-Arabs, they speak their own language, Kurdish. The four Kurds I interviewed were all Muslims (as are the majority of Kurds). There were also three Muslim Turkoman women. (There are Christian and Muslim Turkomans; they live mainly in northern Iraq and also speak their own language.) Finally, three of the women were Christian Arabs.

Whereas the social values, attitudes and behaviour of the non–Arab Muslim minorities might be expected to differ somewhat

15

from those of Arab Muslims, I found their way of thinking, their attitudes and the kind of life they led were very similar to those of Arab Muslims. In fact, the Christians were more rigid than the Muslims, which runs contrary to the popular belief that Christian women in Iraq enjoy greater freedom in their social lives.

Fear of Being Interviewed

Initially, it was difficult to conduct interviews with women in the housewife and teacher categories because of their fears regarding the type of questions asked. Being unfamiliar with this method of research, they were afraid the information might be used against them. People in the Middle East are suspicious and fearful of the authorities and any stranger asking questions might be seen as a government agent. As in many other Middle Eastern societies, Iraqis are not familiar with social statistical data, interviews and questionnaires and they have no appreciation of the value of sociological research. Most of the women I spoke to had either never been interviewed before or had only very limited experience of interviews, so I repeatedly explained the purpose of my investigations and tried to put them at their ease.

Many women were afraid that information might be published which would lead to their husband or a relative being identified: I constantly assured them that they would be given pseudonyms and that all identifying features would be omitted. I varied my approach to suit each woman, trying to make them feel relaxed and comfortable and help them to overcome their inhibitions.

Some of the questions covered taboo subjects in Iraqi society, such as sexuality, and had to be introduced gradually and treated very carefully in order for them to be acceptable. I found it easier to start a conversation with the subject of childhood and socialization than with marital relationships. Thus I opened all interviews with these topics, helping to build a rapport with the women who then felt free to discuss their childhood and express their emotions.

The dialogue was by no means one-sided. The women asked me many questions about my work and especially my married life. Many asked personal favours and wanted my address in London. In general, they were very hospitable, offering me tea, coffee and snacks, or frequently a meal if the interview took place at their home.

Home and the Outside World
The kind of life women lead in the home today does not differ greatly from that in the 1950s. When a girl is transferred from her father's or brother's authority to that of her marriage partner, the husband usually acquires a wife who has been socialized to be submissive, obedient, backward and (until recently) illiterate.

The marital home is a great source of comfort for men, offering them a 'rest centre' for food and sexual intercourse. The wife is expected to look her best upon her husband's return, to have washed and dressed up and to be wearing make-up. Ideally, she has to learn how to be a skilled cook and to keep the house spotlessly clean. All this is done while the husband is away at work or elsewhere. As soon as he enters the home, his wife must attend only to his needs. As far as the children are concerned, it is her duty to produce them, look after them, bring them up in a proper manner and deal with all their problems. The husband is the provider; he does not deal with these everyday matters. Most of his life is led outside the home: at work, with his male friends, in the coffee house, at clubs or at private all-male gatherings.

Historically, these male attitudes to women were reflected in language. Until the early years of this century in some Arabian towns and villages, when a man mentioned a woman's name he would customarily follow it with the words *ajallaka allah*, meaning 'May God put it on a higher level,' a phrase asking for pardon and normally associated with talk of animals.[6] It was an unforgivable crime to ask the actual names of mothers, wives or sisters and might well lead to a quarrel. Government officials frequently came up against men's stubborn refusal to provide the names of their womenfolk when required for official or statistical purposes.

Even today, although women keep their father's name after marriage, they are normally addressed as 'mother of' (Um) coupled with the name of their eldest son, for example, Um Ahmad or Um Muhammad.

Husbands in Iraq do not generally use the word 'my wife' (*marati*) nor do they mention their wife's name or even 'mother of . . .' If they want to be polite, they might address her as 'my folk' (*ahli*) or 'the mother of the boys' (*um al-walad*). On the other hand, some husbands go as far as to address their wives as 'cows' (*haysha*). Or they might say 'my wife' followed by some words of pardon (*tekram*), as if they had just mentioned a hateful or disgusting object. Although these attitudes are disappearing to some extent, they are still found in rural areas and among the poorer classes in cities.

Similar differences between milieux may be observed as regards clothing. The *abaya* (black cloak) is disappearing in the urban sector, particularly among the younger generation. It is still widespread, however, in rural and conservative urban areas and in the holy cities of Najaf and Karbala.

In writing about Yemen, Makhlouf has noted:

> although all the Yemeni female students remain veiled, one can sometimes see incongruous scenes of a veiled girl carrying notebooks chatting with a group of male students, or sitting at a table with boys having a coffee break.[7]

A similar picture is found among female Iraqi university

students, who appear in the latest fashions for their classes and only wear the *abaya* on their way to and from university.[8] Thus for these students, the veil does not necessarily mean seclusion. The same is true for office workers and other women working or studying in a mixed atmosphere.

In the 1960s and early 1970s the young generation of Iraqi girls even adopted the mini skirt, parading in the streets as if the old traditions had never existed. Families could not stop their daughters following the fashion. The authorities used paint to try to stop them and it was a common sight to see policemen with paintbrushes following girls in the street and daubing their legs to try to stop them, to no avail.

There is an important difference between the Iraqi girl and her European counterpart. A European girl will dress up for a special occasion such as a party or a date with her boyfriend, but often dresses simply in her everyday working life. An Iraqi girl, on the other hand, is not free to go out as she chooses, and certainly not with a boyfriend, so she uses elaborate make-up and pays extra attention to her appearance even on ordinary occasions at school or college, in the factory or at the office. Indeed, fashion, clothes and make-up have become almost an obsession with many young urban Iraqi women.[9]

In Iraq today, education and work opportunities for women are encouraged. Education is compulsory for both sexes at primary level (up to approx. 11–12 years). In practice, the majority of girls in urban areas go on to secondary school and many to higher education. Even subjects traditionally considered male preserves such as engineering are open to women at university level.

Most jobs are now also open to women, ranging from lorry- and bus-drivers (due to the need for women's participation in the workforce during the Iraq-Iran war) to doctors, university professors and the top executive positions in ministries. Very few women are in positions of decision-making, however.

A comprehensive national campaign for the eradication of illiteracy has been in force since December 1978. All citizens, male and female, between 15 and 45 years old have by law to attend one of the illiteracy eradication centres found throughout the country. Those who fail to do so are subject to legal measures.

As will be apparent from this book, however, these changes in the areas of work and education have not touched the fundamental issue of women's position within the family and within society.

1
The Pressure to Conform

The Ideology of Honour and Shame

To understand how behaviour is regulated and conduct controlled in Iraqi society, one must understand the Arab concept of honour, which is generally linked to the sexual conduct of women. The dictionary defines honour as 'rules forming conventional standard of conduct'. Pitt-Rivers, writing in 1965, gives a more personal sense: honour is the value of a person in his own eyes.[1] Both these definitions are combined in the Arab concept of honour. But there is more to it than that. Because an Arab represents his kin group, his behaviour must be honourable so that the group are not disgraced. Those who bring shame on their kin are dishonourable. In addition, a man can bring honour both to his kin and to himself by showing generosity or courage, or by having many sons.

But the most important connotation of honour in the Arab world is related to the sexual conduct of women. If a woman is immodest or brings shame on her family by her sexual conduct, she brings shame and dishonour on all her kin. The subtle differences in the notion of honour are reflected in Arabic, which has two words for honour. One, *sharaf*, means honour in the wider sense; the other, *ird*, is linked only with sexual conduct. Someone's honour in the sense of *ird* is so important that he will swear by it like the name of God; a man might swear by the *ird* of his sister, for example. Honour in its more general sense, *sharaf*, can be built up by personal effort, and can be passed on to a person by belonging to an honourable or respectable family.

The phenomenon of 'honour and shame' bears a direct relation to family ties, and to the complex interrelation of social organization and conduct in Arab society. Once a woman breaks the rules, the whole family will be drawn into a sea of shame. An Iraqi proverb states, *al-bint tala ala-umha*, which means, 'The daughter takes after her mother morally.' In other words, the purity of the daughter reflects that of her mother. The family's economic status depends on the father, so the aspect of honour as social status and wealth derives from him, while the aspect of shame derives from the mother. In some cases, losing one's honour is irreparable, while in others it can be regained. Irreparable cases are those when a woman's sexual misconduct becomes public knowledge. Sexual honour is of greater importance than other forms of honour because it is reflected in male circles.

There is another term connected with honour–*aib*, which may be translated as immodesty; a woman who speaks loudly or wears see-through clothes would be considered *aib*, immodest or shameful. In English society, a parent might say to a child, 'Children should be seen and not heard.' Iraqi society uses different words, but the message behind them is very clearly instilled in every girl: it is immodest for a female to laugh or even talk loudly, to argue, and so on. There is a strong social belief that if girls do not learn about immodesty and are not controlled from an early age, they will grow up to bring scandal to their families. We shall return to this point later, after examining some aspects of conduct considered immodest for girls. Thus from a very early age, girls learn what is *aib* and what is not. A girl must not, under any circumstances, be allowed to involve her family in scandal, as this would bring shame on her whole kin group.

When discussing Arab society, the questions arise: Which country are we talking about? And which community? There are many differences between urban and rural areas and between social classes, particularly in the urban sector. However, the phenomenon of honour and shame exists throughout society; its strength merely differs from one community to another. For example, in a traditional sector of society, suspicions of a girl's dishonourable sexual behaviour could result in her being put to death immediately. The same suspicion in a middle-class urban area might result in her being locked indoors while relatives investigated the case. She might be punished by being lectured on morals. The ideology of family honour would be used to transfer guilt onto the girl. She would be watched closely in the future and prevented from going out alone.

Theoretically, people who gossip may damage their reputation. In practice, however, gossip operates as one of the strongest forms of social control, particularly in policing women. Because moral reputation is so important, girls' lives are greatly affected by it. They are very conscious of gossip and any accusation of acting dishonourably. It is important to live up to expectations and they are conditioned to feel this way, in order to be good guardians of the family honour.

The existence of this phenomenon within Iraqi society has meant that women suffer from constant feelings of guilt without necessarily having committed any dishonourable act. Since gossip mainly concerns shame and shameful behaviour, fear of gossip may make parents spy on their children. When discussing her educational history, one of the women I interviewed told me how her family forced her to leave school in order for them to control her more closely. She described her fears and feelings:

I wanted to continue but my father didn't want me to go to school any more. I felt really sad when I finally had to leave school, but on the other hand, I was more relaxed, as I felt uncomfortable outside home. Whenever I left home to go to school, even on the bus, I used to feel somebody was following me, somebody was watching me. I believed that my father wouldn't let me walk alone without asking somebody to observe my movements and report me to him. (*Amina*)

The fear of gossip is based on the fact that a man's honour depends almost entirely on that of the women in his family. Any member of an Arab family not only carries social values with him wherever he goes; he also retains strong family ties even if he starts his own family. Moreover, any dishonourable implication could affect his life quite dramatically. For example, if a man's sister has a questionable reputation, not only would he suffer shame but his own plans for marriage could be sabotaged. Gossip affects a woman's reputation, and therefore her marriage chances. Building a good reputation or losing one's reputation occurs through:

> people's talk (*kalamin nas*). In everything they do, people are forced to consider 'What will people say?' and by this they do not mean 'How will people evaluate and judge?' but 'How might they condemn and distort?' This means that everyone is judged by *some* significant others to be blemished by shame.[2]

If an Arab marries a woman outside his family kin group, his wife will, to some extent, remain a stranger to him and his family, particularly before bearing children. If she were to commit adultery, the shame would be borne by her father's relatives or her mother's male relatives, not her husband's. Any dishonour would reflect upon the husband to a lesser degree, since he can always divorce his wife and disconnect himself from her permanently, unlike her father or brother. It is interesting to note that the person who would have to kill a woman to defend the family honour is usually her brother or father, uncle or cousin. In practice, even her brother-in-law may replace her brother. The husband of a married woman is not expected or indeed allowed to kill her, as members of the family are seen as the possessions of their natal family. Because he is an outsider, a husband cannot perpetrate this act. If a husband were allowed to punish his wife, this would lessen the control of her own family over its members.[3]

This behaviour can work positively too. A woman's brother will try to ensure that his sister's husband treats her properly, because the behaviour of an unhappy woman would reflect badly on her natal family. As a last resort, a divorcee will be accepted back into her family of origin.[4] The following quotation shows a brother's control over his sister:

> I'll never forget an incident which had a great impact on my life. Once, I was peeping through the front door trying to see who was making such a commotion in the street. Suddenly someone hit me from behind, which jabbed the door handle into my eye. I had to be treated in hospital. It was quite painful. My brother was sorry for what he'd done, but he also blamed me for interfering in what was happening outside the house without putting my veil on first. (*Jamila*)

While bearing responsibility for a woman, her family acknowledges that she is their daughter and that she still carries the family name. Out of respect for her paternal family, a woman does not change her name after marriage. This reflects the lack of individualism. The family is always represented by the father's name, because he is the head of the family and the whole family structure is based on him. Consequently, Arab society shows immense respect for the man's image. According to this notion, men are supposed to suffer most from the abuses and shame brought on them by close women relatives, because they feel these women belong to them. They feel responsible for them and control them throughout their lives. In return, they expect women to behave in a respectable manner at all times and under all circumstances–this includes all sexual activities, or any matters considered sexual, such as clothing, movements, and attitudes towards men and even towards women themselves. The ideal married woman is a mother, but one who is virginal in mind and feelings.

A woman who has committed adultery will be referred to as 'the daughter of so and so', using her father's name. In rural areas, and in extreme cases in urban areas, a woman's adultery is punishable by death. The person who revenges his dignity by disposing of the woman who has brought shame upon him and his family will be considered a hero by his fellow men and friends. A new dimension will be added to his pride, ideals and dignity. In order to preserve the honourable name of the family or tribe, men must control their women or be killed for failing to exercise such control.[5]

Attitudes towards Girls

Although Islam forbade the ancient practice of *al-waad*, or female infanticide, the persecution of girls has persisted, mainly due to the continued existence of the honour-shame ideology.

Arab society was, and remains, largely agricultural. In rural areas, the need for field workers remains very important, and as men are considered to be more physically able than women, the need for sons fuels the historical hatred of women. However, both in areas where women do the majority of work in the fields (particularly in southern Iraq) and in urban areas where there is little need for hard labour, the negative attitude towards baby girls remains much the same.

Differentiation between males and females starts even before birth. A phrase frequently used to congratulate a newly married couple is, 'We wish you prosperity and sons.' When a woman becomes pregnant, she will hope, throughout her pregnancy, for a boy. If the baby is a girl, everybody she knows will pity her and feel unhappy for her.[6] In Iraq when people visit the mother of a baby girl, they frequently say, 'It's all right. The womb which held a girl will hold a boy next.' Or, if they are trying to be considerate, and the attitude of the in-laws threatens to become hostile, they might say, 'Never mind. At least the mother's all right.' The scientific fact that it is the male who determines the sex of the child is generally unknown in Iraq, even among educated people. Women are still divorced by their husbands on the grounds that they can only have daughters.[7]

Attitudes to the birth of a baby boy are reflected in the words of the Palestinian poet Rashid Hussein:

The main thing they care about is to see the wife giving birth to a baby boy,
So they will say, 'She is the daughter of an honourable man whom we are all proud of.'
She gave birth to a baby boy,
his face is just like a moon.[8]
They will say, 'Her husband is a great masculine man.'

In trying to discover more about social attitudes towards baby girls, I first asked the women what they could remember from their own childhood and their own families about the birth of girls. Most had been emotionally affected by being born female and many wept when recalling their parents. This may be because their childhood was unhappy, or conversely because some loved relative from those days was now dead. The following comments illustrate their feelings:

27

My mother had five daughters and then had sons. Her in-laws wanted to find another wife for my father because of that. But thank God she had sons later on. (*Fatin*)

When my mother had a baby girl, people told her, 'Never mind, the important thing is that you're all right,' but when she had a son they sacrificed a sheep for her, and everybody showed their happiness at the event. (*Khadija*)

I have one brother and one sister. My mother felt bad when she had a baby girl, and she wasn't alone in this; my aunt and everybody else felt upset too. Even me, when my first daughter was born, I said, 'It's all right, I do have a son,' but the third child was a disaster. I had all three of my children by Caesarean section, so I hadn't quite come round from the anaesthetic when I heard my sister telling me I had a beautiful girl that looked just like Udday, my son. I screamed 'Yaboooo' [an exclamation of shock] and fainted. (*Zahida*)

My mother had six children: three boys and three girls. When she had the last child–the third baby girl–my uncle was so angry, he beat my mother, causing her grievous bodily harm which resulted in her death a few months later. (*Labiba*)

To tell you the truth, people generally feel bad about the birth of a girl, and they sympathise with the mother. For example, a few weeks ago, one of our teachers had a baby girl. When her husband came to school to collect her salary and told us the news, the staff reacted in similar ways. One of them said, 'Oh, no. I don't know what to say, poor thing!' Another said, 'Never mind, we hope you'll have a boy next time.' We didn't stop these remarks until we realized that the man was very embarrassed. Of course, we didn't mean to embarrass him, but we loved her and the news was very bad. Mind you, that was her third girl. If it had been the first, we wouldn't have minded as much. Anyway, he left us without uttering a single word, and later on we asked her to apologize to him for our odd behaviour. She understood. She knew we cared. (*Nazira*)

Girls cause problems. That's why a girl's family feels sorry at her birth. (*Majida*)

Girls are oppressed. That's why people feel sad at a girl's birth. They feel sorry for her. (*Amina*)

I have one sister and five brothers. Nevertheless my mother hated girls. When I first got married, my husband and I made a decision to have four children, but he made it clear that I ought to have at least two sons. This changed everything in our lives. I had to have six children, because I had four daughters first. (*Jumana*)

A baby boy is highly valued in Arab society and because people are superstitious and believe in the evil eye, they think other people, whether envious or not, can cause harm and endanger the baby's life; even an admiring look from the mother might harm the baby unless it is followed by a phrase from the Quran. Sometimes even praising a baby might harm it. Iraqis normally use the protective phrase, *imhassan ib allah* before praising a baby.

A boy's family will often dress him as a girl and call him by a girl's name, or even pierce his ears or let his hair grow. By doing this they believe that evil will overlook such a worthless creature, because it is female. Many people hang a talisman in the boy's bedding or clothing, believing the charm will attract the evil eye when it glances at the baby and that the talisman will suck all the evil from this first glance. The second glance contains no evil and the child will not be harmed. These fears continue for approximately the first five years of life, after which the boy is considered strong enough for the evil eye to no longer harm him.[9]

Boys are an added qualification for social prestige. The parents of male children will often adopt their eldest son's name, particularly in public and sometimes even at home–they will be known as Abu [father of] Muhammad and Um [mother of] Muhammad, for example. A mother will not be called by her own name or her daughter's. She will not even be regarded as a mother (which means gaining relatively better status) until her first son is born.[10] Women who bear no children are called Um Khaieb, meaning 'mother of [the] absent', but still in the male gender. It is possible to know people by their children's names for years without ever knowing their real names, since they are always acknowledged as 'mother of so-and-so' or 'father of so-and-so' after their sons.[11] The discrimination between boys and girls exists even in lullabies. A common Iraqi lullaby goes, *deliloy yal walad yabni deliloy*, meaning 'la la la, my little boy'. It is addressed to a baby boy, rather than a baby girl. Most mothers sing this song to their babies regardless of sex.

There are many reasons for not welcoming the birth of a baby girl. Perhaps the most important is the fact that bringing up boys is much easier than bringing up girls, since whatever boys do, their conduct will affect only themselves, rather than the family, as is the case with girls. These fears of having a baby girl have historical origins, stemming from the fact that honour was the main issue in a girl's life. Since honour demands that girls be watched closely and controlled, their upbringing is fraught with difficulties.

Whereas men are supposed to be tough, rational and independent, women are brought up to be emotional and submissive. This socialization process strengthens the bond between the woman and her family, denying her any independence beyond the family unit, and so she always remains her family's responsibility. If a woman's husband dies or she is divorced, the natal family is responsible for her welfare and that of her children, and has legal custody over them until they reach a certain age. In the event of divorce, the woman is expected to return to her family with custody of the children until they reach a certain age, as long as the father does not claim custody of them. Thus families see even an infant girl as potentially a lifelong responsibility.

Growing up Female–the Concept of Femininity

Next I wanted to explore social attitudes towards the female child and what growing up as a female means in Iraqi society. Among the issues that contribute to a girl's socialization are the family name, obedience, chastity and puberty.

The Family Name

In Iraq, a son holds the family name and passes it on to his own children. The children of a daughter, however, take their father's name, although the woman retains her own family name after marriage. Thus a wife's family name cannot pass through her offspring to the next generation. The idea of immortality is invoked when people offer their best wishes by saying to a man, 'May your offspring not be discontinued until doomsday.' This saying can be interpreted as a desire for further male children. Another important factor connected with name and strength in numbers can be found in traditional tribal customs: the more members in a tribe, the stronger they are.

Obedience

In the process of socializing girls to fit the 'feminine stereotype', the most important issue for the mother–and other adults in the family–is how to make them totally submissive. A girl is taught to be obedient from an early age and will be punished if she refuses to do what adults in the family demand of her. It is *aib* (shameful, immodest) for her to disobey, although it is not necessarily *aib* for a boy. When a boy wants to join in an adult conversation, it will be tolerated, but not for a girl–this would be considered very *aib*.

The differential treatment of boys and girls within the family affects their personalities–the ways in which family members behave towards them conditions them to fill different roles in life and have different expectations. In order to fit ideas of manhood, boys are taught to treat younger children as inferior, though ill-treatment of young children is not acceptable from girls, who should always be kind and calm. Whereas boys are taught to be strong and not to be afraid, girls are constantly reminded of fear, and of their physical weakness. They are expected to control themselves and their needs and not be demanding; they should wait until things are offered to them, except in case of necessity, when they should ask very politely. Boys, on the other hand, are taught to demand what they want and ask for it directly. When a girl cries, she is either told to stop or ignored. But the boy is told that a big, strong boy never cries and that he should not be *imkhanath*, or 'sissy'. While boys are encouraged to play rough games, climb trees, play out of doors and learn how to defend themselves, girls are conditioned to act in a totally opposite manner.

Since honour is linked with women's sexual conduct, a girl's appearance and the way she dresses are very important, and strict adherence to the prescribed standard is demanded. This is particularly true of games and sports. Girls are constantly reminded to be careful how they talk or move, to avoid their skirt riding up when they sit and to avoid crossing their legs. They are not allowed to wear tight or revealing clothes and are taught never to meet the eyes of strangers.

Girls are discouraged from activities preferred by boys, who always have first choice in everything. If a boy gets into a fight with other children, he is usually told, 'Never mind. You're a boy,' but a girl would be punished. Girls should not raise their voices, answer their elders back or indulge in the types of activities encouraged in their male counterparts. They should not mix with other children living in their area, as good girls always stay at home. All of these actions would be considered as corrupting moral values; girls should be shy and polite. If a girl does not follow these unwritten laws, her family will fear for her future, as she might bring shame on them one day. An interesting sidelight is thrown on this issue by women's attitude to smoking. Just because smoking is always known as male conduct, the women I interviewed considered it shameful for women to smoke.

I asked the women about their own experience within their natal families, whether they were restricted in the way they dressed or behaved, and whether they had heard the word *aib* and in what sense. The following answers are typical:

We used to hear the word *aib*, 'Do not go out alone,' 'Do not laugh loudly,' 'Do not sit with visitors.' You know, I used to serve tea or whatever my mother wanted me to serve for visitors, and run out the minute I'd finished, particularly if they were married women. Mother didn't want us to listen to their conversation. We thought these instructions were incontestable. (*Haifa*)

If you want me to count the do's and don't's, the list would go on for ever. It seems that everything is *aib* for girls. (*Ibtihal*)

When I reached the age of 12, they prevented me from going out. This was a big change in my life because I still wanted to play with children in the street. (*Amina*)

My mother used to insist on giving me lectures on how to behave. I didn't like them then, but believed that it was for my own good. (*Gamila*)

It should be stressed that many women take pride in being obedient, whether as daughters or wives. By doing only what is expected of them, they avoid even greater restrictions:

They didn't pressurize us because we used to follow the line they planned for us. (*Lutfia*)

They used to tell us not to stand by the outside front door, not to laugh loudly and not to wear short skirts. We did everything they said, so we had no problems whatsoever with our parents. (*Ibtihal*)

I didn't do anything wrong that might lead to complaints from the family. I didn't go out or mix with people, and I wear acceptable clothes. (*Feryal*)

Mothers, fathers, brothers or other adults controlling girls within the family all work towards the same end: to protect male honour within the family.

Virginity and Chastity
The Arabic word *adhra* (virgin) is a feminine word always used to refer to women, never to men; there is no masculine equivalent. When some of the women told me that their husbands 'had no sexual experience before marriage', they had no convenient masculine term to use.
   A girl who loses her virginity is liable to be punished with physical or 'moral' death; the latter involves isolation and virtual house arrest. If, on the wedding day, she was found not to be a

virgin she would be divorced. Such a divorce is, of course, accompanied by *fadiha* (scandal). If it is not restricted to family circles, such scandal often spreads dramatically. Such a girl may be completely innocent of any sexual relation, but have no way of proving her innocence. Nawal El Saadawi describes the experience of a woman who was born with a non-perforated hymen; this caused her abdomen to swell because her menstrual flow had accumulated in her vagina for months. She needed a small operation to let the fluid out. Her husband accused her of not being a virgin, 'since she had not bled from the external genital organs on the night of the marriage'.[12] Various minor abnormalities can result in a young woman appearing not to have an intact hymen. Because such enormous importance is placed on virginity, many women consult doctors before marriage to ensure that their hymen is still inact.

In this context we should mention the 'honour crime', in which a relative kills a woman who has been found in an illicit sexual relationship. The official punishment for the male who commits such a crime is lenient and in fact discretionary. Such crimes have always occurred more frequently in rural and bedouin areas, and among less educated people. Although most of the women I spoke to had never heard directly of any such crime actually occurring, the fact that they are known to occur inspires fear in all Iraqi women.

An Iraqi feminist poet describes the case of a woman 'wiped out in blood':

Dawn will come and the girls will ask about her,
Where is she? and the monster will answer:
'We killed her.'
A mark of shame was on our forehead and we washed it off.

Her black tale will be told by neighbours,
And will be told in the quarter even by the palm trees,
Even the wooden doors will not forget her,
It will be whispered even by the stones.
Washing off the shame . . . Washing off the shame.
O neighbours, O village girls,
Bread we shall knead with our tears.

We'll shear our plaits and skin our hands,
To keep their clothes white and pure,
No smile, no joy, no turn as the knife so waiting
For us in the hand of father or brother
And tomorrow, who knows which desert
Swallows us, to wash off shame?[13]

By tracing the stages of a girl's life, we can see that she is
unwelcome from the moment of birth. Compared with her
brothers, she grows up relatively neglected. She is seen as part of
the household until she reaches the age of puberty, when suddenly
the spotlight is on, and everyone in the family changes their way
of dealing with her. The family impose a list of compulsory
behaviour, which regulates her every movement both inside and
outside the home; they prevent her from mixing with boys,
dictate the type of clothes she wears, and so on. I tried to find out
from the women I interviewed how much personal freedom they
had, and how their upbringing had shaped their personalities.
Here are some typical comments:

I didn't have a choice in what to wear. My father was very
conservative. He didn't allow us to wear short dresses at the
time when they were fashionable in the early sixties. They
didn't allow me to visit my friends. However, they allowed
them to visit me. (*Wafaa*)

They were generous and allowed me to give my opinion about the clothes I wore, provided they were not sleeveless or short and see-through. Visiting friends was totally forbidden. (*Sawsan*)

I didn't have a choice in my marriage. How could they possibly give me a choice in what to wear? They didn't allow me to mix with people. Mother said we'd learn bad things from mixing. (*Amal*)

I was satisfied with whatever they bought me. Social life, friends and hobbies were out of the question, as I had no spare time. My mother had so many children younger than me that I had to look after, and also my homework to do. That was before they forced me to leave school. (*Amina*)

I was free to choose what I wore and free to choose my friends, but my visits were restricted to one friend because her family was trustworthy. Nevertheless, mother didn't mind too much when other friends visited me, provided I gave her some information about them and their families. (*Fadwa*)

It is obvious from these answers that the girls lacked outside support and connections, because they were prevented by their families from experiencing them. By confining the girls to the house and restricting and supervising visitors, it was much easier to exercise control.

The implication of this traditional outlook is that Iraqi society itself can change little because each individual will think she is on her own with her grievances. Group movements will not develop. In the West, by contrast, it is the friends of teenage girls who play a large part in supporting and socializing them. Strong friendships develop as the girls spend long periods together, sometimes travelling and taking holiday jobs together. The families have a relaxed and accepting attitude to this practice.

Puberty

El Saadawi, writing from her own experience of menstruation, states:

> No one, with the exception of women, can imagine what this young girl would feel. She wakes up in the morning to see flowing red blood between her legs. I still remember the white colour of my face in the mirror on that dark morning. My lips were white and blue. My arms and legs were shivering. I thought the disaster I had feared was taking place, and a stranger had assaulted me in my bedroom and caused that damage. That was one of my worries, and I used to close my bedroom windows before going to sleep.[14]

This traumatic description of the onset of menstruation is very similar to that of many of the women I interviewed. Since girls are taught that the loss of virginity is symbolized by a few drops of blood, menstruation can be a terrifying experience. The intense fear experienced by girls who imagine that they have lost their virginity is difficult to describe.

More than half the women I spoke to said they had had no prior knowledge of menstruation. The shock they experienced was described in graphic detail:

> At the age of 13 I used to mingle with our servants and listen to their conversations. One of their favourite topics of gossip concerned pregnancy and birth. From listening to them I learned about menstruation. It bothered my mother when she saw me with them. There were so many unanswered questions in my mind then, but I felt ashamed to ask my mother about

them, so I couldn't talk about my sudden period. I can only say that I felt uncomfortable, and found answers after marriage. (*Salwa*)

Only four of the women had been told about menstruation in advance by their mother or an older sister; several others had overheard servants' conversations or learned from friends. The information gained from friends and acquaintances (which is often unreliable) can have a dramatic effect on the minds of young girls:

This experience is very painful to recall. I blame my mother for it. My first period was a sad occasion; I cried for two days and was terribly scared. My mother reassured me, saying it was quite a normal thing to happen, but I was sure it was something abnormal. (*Haifa*)

I lived in fear for the first three months. I felt as if I'd committed an offence. I feared people and society. Then I gradually revealed my feelings to my class-mates, which put an end to my suffering and worries. (*Nazira*)

The experience of menstruation offers an insight into the ways mothers and daughters relate to each other: only very few of the women had prior knowledge of it from their mothers. Many indicated that their mothers were too shy to discuss it with them, even after they had approached them in fear and trembling, desperately in need of reassurance and advice:

I was shivering with fear when I ran to mother to tell her. She said, 'It's all right,' and told me what I should do. In short, she was too shy to talk about it in detail. (*Lutfia*)

I was surprised and shocked. When I told my mother, she only said, 'Oh, you poor thing.' (*Jamila*)

Khawla's mother was also too shy to talk to her:

I was 12 years old when my periods started. I overheard some girls talking about it at school, but was too shy to ask. When I started, I didn't go to my mother, I was too shy, but she noticed some blood on my nightgown. She came to me, very worried, and asked, 'Did you jump down from a high place? Has anyone seduced you? Tell me the truth.' When I answered no, she said, 'Don't worry. It's only your period.'

Zahida had an even more frightening experience:

I was 13 years old when my periods started. I was so afraid, I was hysterical; I had to go to my mother. She started asking me whether a man had come near me, if I'd fallen down, and so on; I told her I didn't think so. Although she told me what to do and tried to calm me down, I was still very scared, I think because I'd seen my aunt having her baby. She was visiting us when she started labour and while my mother rushed out to get the midwife, the baby was almost born and I saw it all. Somehow from what little I knew about the whole subject of pregnancy, I thought when I got my period that what had happened to my aunt was happening to me; I don't know why I connected them together. Funnily enough, when my younger sister came to me to ask my advice when her period started, I asked her exactly what my mother had asked me: 'Did you fall down? Have you been carrying something heavy? Has a man touched you?'

Mothers and Daughters
Since the mother's role is to bring her daughters up according to

the values and standards of society, she herself must not adopt any constructively critical attitudes towards those standards. In order to fulfil her duty of socializing her daughters, the mother does not allow herself to become too close to them. Just as there are no terms of endearment between herself and her husband and family, so there are no terms of endearment between any of the adult members of the family. Nor in everyday life is there much physical embracing, particularly after childhood, except at special celebrations. The mother and daughter might do household tasks together, such as sewing or cooking, but it is an unequal relationship, more like that of teacher and pupil. They do not play games together, and their outings are with the whole family, attending family events or having picnics in a family group. They might go shopping together but it is unlikely that they would have coffee tête-à-tête.

Thus the chances of a one-to-one relationship developing are extremely remote. In previous generations there were so many children that, apart from family events, it was not possible for the mother to spend her leisure with them. Women today work too hard to have time or energy to spend with their children, apart from carrying out the necessary tasks. In addition, there is a generation gap, perpetuated by older people who wish to keep separate and remote, so that they can better control the younger generation. (It is always the older women who control the younger ones.) And in Iraq it is not only the mother and older sisters, but also perhaps a grandmother and aunts who live in the natal home, who will be trying to control the daughter.

Most of the women I interviewed showed by their answers that they had kept to the rules set down for them, thus avoiding confrontation with their parents. In such circumstances, many girls prefer to leave the parental home by marrying–regardless of the type of man they have as a partner. The most important consideration is to be free of parental control. As one of the women said, when I asked why she married, 'One gets married to get away from home, don't you agree?' I then asked, 'How would you say you got on with your mother?' The following are typical of their answers:

My mother had a very weak personality and her behaviour was pessimistic and discouraging, so there was no real understanding between us. (*Suha*)

I love my mother but I don't like the way she brought us up. She worried so much about our reputation and always warned us about this or that . . . It seems that all she had to teach us was how to protect the family honour. (*Bahira*)

My mother was a good woman. She was strict sometimes, but for our own good. (*Muna*)

We were very obedient. Mother was too strict. We didn't like it then, but I now believe she was right. (*Majida*)

My relationship with my mother was friendly and sympathetic but I didn't like her frequent complaints at home, as she didn't do anything about what was wrong apart from complaining. (*Fatin*)

Despite my mother's inexperience, she was rough and bad-tempered with us. We lived in an environment of threats and tension. (*Suhad*)

My mother was unhappy in her life. She hated herself and she used to vent her anger on us. She never taught us the difference between right and wrong. (*Jumana*)

Most women felt sorry for their mothers, as they recognized that they were leading unhappy lives; the reasons for this will be explored later in this chapter.

Because their mothers were totally submissive to their husbands, most of the women lacked any model of a strong female character on which to base their behaviour. Consequently, despite the fact that they all criticized their mothers, they also admired them and tried to follow their example. This is a good illustration of the conflict between behavioural patterns instituted within the home and those learned from outside, as all of them were aware of their mothers' submissive status. However, the teaching within the home remained stronger than any outside influences.

It is clear that a child's experience will vary according to the rewards or punishments its mother metes out and these rewards or punishments vary according to parental expectations. These expectations, in turn, are based on the gender designation of the child. Because a girl is often rewarded for being submissive and obedient, she will tend to develop a passive or negative personality. The family will make decisions about every area of her life: what she eats, the clothes she wears, how she spends her time, and also more important matters such as education and marriage. So girls continue to play similar roles to their mothers, because their socialization continues to enforce the same values. The following quotation illustrates this point:

> I wasn't allowed to visit my friends because it would be shameful to meet their brothers by chance. They frightened me. They gave us the impression that we could get pregnant just by sitting next to boys. I used to sleep far away from my brothers on the roof. They were right in a sense. A girl shouldn't have a loud voice and she shouldn't laugh in the street. I'm still bothered by my daughter's behaviour when she

tries to comb her hair in the car. Of course, this 'shame' doesn't apply to boys. They say men can carry their 'shame' with them. When I was 12 or 13 I was frightened to go to the bathroom. I had to wipe and wash everything thoroughly in the bathroom, particularly if my father or brothers had used it before me. (*Jumana*)

Once a girl marries, however, her relationship with her mother seems to improve and they can become more like friends–this applies to women from all classes. A mother feels it is her duty to teach her daughter how to look after her marriage and deal with any problems that might occur. She might teach her ways of wearing make-up and how to look after her figure. After marriage a daughter will tell her mother all about her private affairs, seeking her advice in order to strengthen her marriage. If she works, she may accept her mother's help with the housework or children, so the two women become very close. Since the girl's virginity is no longer an issue, the restrictions on her behaviour can be relaxed and the relationship also becomes more open.[15]

Parents and Daughters
Family affairs seem to be a painful topic of discussion. The women's comments were brief and sometimes contradictory, especially regarding the more involved family relationships. Some tried to avoid talking about these by giving short answers, such as 'Not bad' or 'All right', to my questions, 'How would you say your parents get on together?', 'Are there any difficulties between them?' However, most answered the questions after some deliberation. Only a few described their parents' relationship as 'good'; the majority unhesitatingly described it as 'bad', with the father 'fussy', 'bad-tempered' and 'violent' and the mother 'obedient', 'submissive', 'tormented', 'deprived' and 'unhappy'.

From all their responses a picture emerges of family life and how the fathers behaved. Men would often complain about their meals being too salty or not cooked properly. They might say the house would fall apart from the amount of cleaning done. If the mother tried to make her husband aware of her needs, he would say that she was nagging him, or would tell her to take the children away, so that he could get some rest. If the mother's friends happened to come round, he would say 'Not again!' and make negative and rude comments about them. The father, by contrast, would bring friends home for dinner without any warning. Husbands would be consistently late for dinner or not come home at all. One woman's mother complained of having to spend all her life waiting around for her husband, as he was late for everything. Another woman described how her drunken father would make a habit of dismantling the garden wall, brick by brick, when he came in after a drinking session. Most women who gave a negative picture of family relationships attributed this to the 'assumed superiority' of the male over the female, and to the strongly enforced standards of sexual practice in Iraq. Women remembered seeing their fathers breaking things, shouting and hitting the children and sometimes even the mother. All this is due to control being exercised through an exaggerated concept of 'masculinity'.

Mothers may also exaggerate their problems and their reactions in order to get from their children the love and attention that are lacking in their marital relationships. This may explain why many of the women felt so sorry for their mothers. The way parents treat each other has a direct effect on a child's personality. The father is the authoritarian figure in the family, while the mother can in no way reach his level of authority. The lower her educational level, the weaker her position in relation to her husband and the greater the conflict produced in the children, who will be forced to take sides. They usually take the mother's side, because in most cases they see the father as the aggressor. A boy may wish to exercise the authority that has been instilled in him, and try to control the household when his father is away; thus a brother can also be a source of fear for his sister, in addition to the father and other male relatives. The unhappiness experienced by a young girl when her parents' relationship deteriorates can lead to great psychological harm and confusion as she tries to understand and accept life. Consequently, girls tend to grow up carrying the enormous burden of an unfulfilled childhood. Needless to say, the parents' marital relationship will have a direct influence on that of their children.

In many of the cases I studied it seemed that while the father behaved reasonably and considerately outside the home, his behaviour within the family unit was often overbearing and aggressive. (This may explain the way that the women saw other men.[16]) One explanation for this dual standard of behaviour is a man's desire to exercise authority over his wife and children and be a *rijjal hok*, meaning a 'macho man'. As discussed earlier, this attitude is reinforced by socialization as mothers encourage their male children from a very early age to fit into so-called 'manhood'. Another explanation might be that the men have problems outside the home related to their jobs, for example, and they take it out on their wives.

As it is socially acceptable for Arab men to show irritable, angry behaviour, the atmosphere in the home is often highly charged, fraught and quarrelsome.[17] At all-male gatherings, men tend to be aggressive and quarrelsome. If a man is aggressive in the street, this may lead to a general fight. In the case of a car accident, the drivers might get out and start punching each other. Men also tend to make loud sexual comments about any woman in the street who is not veiled or who wears revealing clothes. This behaviour is most common among poor, uneducated people. When educated men need to release their aggressive feelings they do so mainly at home. Women, on the other hand, are generally discouraged from expressing their anger with their men, so they transfer their pent-up emotions by exercising control over their children. This also applies to older women controlling younger women within the family. Such patterns are changing, however, and many wives can now be seen shouting at their husbands.[18]

In analysing the women's answers as they compared their parents' relationships with their own, I discovered many similarities. Most of the women said their mothers were obedient and submissive. Although they criticized male power within the family, whether from fathers or husbands, they still saw women's submissiveness as a good quality. When talking about their parents, the women observed:

Although my father married my mother when she was very young and beautiful, plus being an excellent housewife and obedient, he didn't take good care of her and didn't take her out. Once a year at least he goes abroad for a holiday but never in their married life has he taken her along with him. She feels that he doesn't respect her and that she has no status as she should in a family. (*Fatin*)

Mother is obedient. She never argues, so they live in peace. (*Suad*)

They have a very good relationship. The minute he gets home he calls for her. She's a very good housewife, and obedient, and when he arrives home she leaves all the housework and gives him her full attention. (*Feryal*)

Although Suad did not wish to discuss her parents' relationship, she ended our conversation by saying that her father was educated, and so he had a good relationship with her mother. Others, however, indicated just the opposite:

47

Father looked down on mother, and always complained that she had no education and was not a modern woman. He used to get drunk every day. As a reaction, she turned to religion and kept to herself. (*Huda*)

They didn't have a good relationship. He always felt that he was superior, more educated; he looked down on her as she was illiterate. I used to feel terrified when he accused her of being stupid and threatened to remarry, particularly after he'd been drinking. She served him and us all her life, but she was extremely unhappy, dissatisfied and irritable. (*Fadwa*)

We must remember that the daughters who made these negative comments belong to the first generation influenced by the media and Westernization. In reality, not all the mothers may have felt that their marriages were as brutal and empty as they appeared to the daughters. Thus if a father were to bring fruit home in the evening, this might please his wife in a way that the daughter would not understand. Another common practice in that generation was for the husband to buy a piece of gold jewellery for his wife. Though he might see it as an investment, and the children might also see it that way, the wife would look upon it as a present and an addition to her own property. In general, the women indicated that not only were their mothers submissive, but their fathers were often violent, fussy and bad-tempered. The following are some examples:

They were always quarrelling. She was always working at home. Despite that, he wanted to have a clean, tidy home and nice meals, all the time. He wanted her to put a nice dress on and not do the housework but pay attention only to him whenever he was at home. But she couldn't really afford the time. (*Nazira*)

Mother feels tormented and deprived with him. He used to leave her every night to go out and drink with his friends. (*Suha*)

There wasn't any understanding between them. When I was little I remember that he even used to beat her. She really suffered a lot. (*Sawsan*)

My father was bad-tempered and fussy. We suffered from that a lot; we felt sorry for our mother. (*Suhad*)

My father beats my mother, but not as often as he shouts and swears at her. He even throws her out sometimes and she goes to her parents, but he brings her back a few days later, or sometimes her family does. He's an alcoholic. When he drinks he gets worse, but she's had to accept all that and be patient just for us. (*Rahima*)

My father's very fussy. If the food is a little salty or something, he gets mad. She just accepts that and always remains silent. (*Wafaa*)

I was 4 years old when my mother died, but I know from the family that my father tormented her. (*Labiba*)

Most women told me that their mothers were extremely unhappy because of their husbands' attitude and behaviour. Some thought it was quite normal for men to be irritable and that their mothers coped well. A few said their fathers used to beat their wives. Many pointed out that their fathers were alcoholic, or at least frequent drinkers. The fact that these men drink shows their lack of respect for religion, as alcohol is prohibited by Islam.[19] As mentioned earlier, the women described their fathers' irritable behaviour and that of their husbands in very similar terms. The mothers, however, apart from feelings of unhappiness, seemed to regard themselves as cursed by fate. These attitudes are similar to their daughters'. For example, Madiha said her mother used to:

> curse the fate which led her to marry him, but she was hoping to be rewarded with her children.

And Sabiha cursed:

> the one who was the reason for our marriage despite the fact that he's my cousin.

A Daughter's Education

I asked all the women about their parents' plans and wishes for their daughters' education and careers. I also asked the housewives why they had left school or whether they had gone to school at all. Several indicated that their parents had not allowed them even to start school. Others had started school only to leave after one to three years. The main reason for leaving school was to help their mothers with the housework, as they were either the oldest girl in the family or had an older sister who had married. This can be seen as a side issue, however, compared to that of honour and shame. One of the working women explained:

> In our time there wasn't as strong a reason for the girl to study as there is now. People were asking my father why my older sister was still at school. When he asked her to leave school he asked me to do so too. As he put it, 'Either they go to school together or they stay at home together.' I didn't mind because the same thing happened to my sister. I wasn't very happy at school. We had to cross a very dangerous bridge on the way there. I also liked staying in bed in the morning. When I got

older I asked to go back to school and did very well, because while I was at home I'd gone through a lot of my father's books. (*Najwa*)

Many of the working women had attended school and college with the approval of their parents. However, some had to study subjects in which they were not interested in order to gain this approval. Parental disapproval of a daughter's choice of subject was usually related to honour rather than any wish for the daughter to take up a better subject. For example, Haifa's wish to take a secretarial course at college was not approved by her father, simply because he did not want her to work as a secretary for 'someone' in future. In his mind, no respectable girl would apply for such a job. It was not that the father viewed the subject as worthless; rather, he feared for the loss of his daughter's honour. The following examples illustrate this point:

They encouraged me to study but refused to let me study engineering which was my preference. In 1959 I finished high school in Egypt with very good grades and wanted to study engineering, since engineering and medicine were reserved for those with high grades and were considered the top two specialist subjects. However, I didn't get a place at Baghdad University. Two of my sisters were studying medicine but I didn't like it. The original idea was to study in Beirut as an alternative but my father and mother refused. They said, 'Engineering, and on top of that abroad!' So I studied management and economics. I liked my studies and finished successfully. I went on to get an MA in management from the American University in Beirut. (*Baidaa*)

I went for an interview at the Department of English Studies since this was my parents' wish. I wanted to study physical education, especially as my college tutors encouraged me to do so. When I told my parents about it, they totally rejected the idea, so I studied English. (*Wafaa*)

I wanted to study law or journalism. English was my last choice. Father didn't agree and told me I had to study English. It wasn't a big disappointment for me as I didn't mind studying English, especially as I knew my father well: he would never have let me go to court and things like that. (*Maisoon*)

The system of higher education is inflexible for both sexes. Students need very high marks to qualify for university places in particular subjects. If a girl gets the required marks and is then barred by her family from starting the course she wants, this will lead to great frustration, which may affect her studies and her whole subsequent career. A happy woman in a career of her own choice would reflect on her family, and the opposite is also true. Most of the women I interviewed had not been free to choose their career.

Life for Children Today

Despite the spread of education among urban women, their attitudes towards children have changed little. Whereas today's children have toys and material possessions that their parents did not, they are not necessarily happier. In the past, living in extended families, they could play freely with other children. Nowadays the nuclear family system makes this much more difficult. In addition, mothers are always busy with their own work and housework, and do not play with their children; they cannot even see why it is necessary. The relationship with the father is even worse, as he hardly sees his children at home.

When children begin to walk and talk at around the age of 2, they face a form of oppression called *tawjeh*, or discipline. They repeatedly hear, 'Don't do this', 'Don't do that,' 'This is *aib*, that is *haram*' (meaning wrong and forbidden), all without explanation. The child who asks questions will get very short answers, if any. When they wish to disagree or refuse to do something, children use the only weapon they have: tears. The reason for this treatment is that children are not seen as normal human beings who can understand what is explained to them. When a child cries the mother normally offers sweets, toys or kisses, although she knows the child will be punished by the father or another member of the family. In other words, adults frequently contradict each other's actions towards their children, often in their presence.

Girls are normally treated more harshly than boys, however, as a girl must not learn to get her own way; she must be controlled from a very early age to ensure her future. Due to the age hierarchy, parents commonly give children commands rather than explaining. Thus children do not grow up to make their own decisions and develop as independent people, and this obviously has negative consequences for society as well as for themselves. When they grow up, girls tend to regard crying as a weapon; this makes their marital relationship manipulative rather than affectionate and honest.

This socializing takes other forms with boys. They are taught that they should not cry like girls. They learn instead how to shout 'like a man' and threaten to get what they want, despite any hardship this might cause the family. When their sons behave like this, most mothers see it as a 'phase' and tell themselves it will pass. They tend to believe that a teenage boy is only frustrated in his desire for a woman, and that unless they treat him indulgently he might go mad. It is a common belief in Arab society that to frustrate a man's sexual desires will result in madness. So mothers are lenient towards their sons, who may seek sexual relief by going to prostitutes, for example, even though the mothers may be shocked and disgusted by this behaviour.

The disciplining of children is not solely the job of parents, but also that of relatives, particularly grandparents, uncles, aunts, and society as a whole. Neighbours and other people might also participate, in the belief that they are helping the parents. At school, teachers play an important role, using many kinds of orders to discipline children without having to offer any explanation. Children are taught not to argue with their teachers, but to show them an exaggerated degree of respect.[20]

Children are brought up to respect teachers not only on account of their profession, but also because they are regarded as older and wiser and therefore worthy of respect. Children frequently hear the saying, *akbar mennak yom aakal mennak sena*, meaning, 'He who is one day older than you is in fact wiser by one year.' Inevitably, such an upbringing severely restricts both girls and boys, although girls suffer more from it. It also affects the personality of both sexes. Children are not taught to think for themselves, or to develop their creativity and individuality. Later on they tend to blame other people for what goes wrong in their life. Instead of self-reliance, people are taught to rely on the family in every way. But in many cases the family and other older people will not be there when support is needed; people who have always relied on the wisdom and support of others will then find it very difficult to deal with situations within their marriage and in society. Paradoxically, those people who themselves found it hard to take responsibility will have to take responsibility for younger people in their turn.

Differentiation between boys and girls is concerned mainly with attitudes and behaviour, in connection with morals and the ideology of honour and shame, rather than with material things. From my fieldwork, general observations and personal experience, it appears very unlikely that boys will be given better food or nicer clothes than those of their sisters, for example.

The situation for girls is particularly difficult. Girls are rejected from the day they are born. Thus they are strictly controlled, and grow up in an atmosphere of fear and questioning, with their every word and movement constantly observed. They endure all these problems to protect their honour, and in order to lead a 'normal' life by getting married. Such an achievement requires, above all, a good reputation, which is something every girl and her family have to nurture with care. The reward for a good reputation is marriage.

2
'Choosing' a Partner

The institution of marriage is of the utmost importance in the Arab world, particularly among Muslims. Marriage is specifically encouraged by Islam, by society and by most Arab governments. In addition the natal family encourages marriage for boys and girls of a marriageable age. (The older women are especially concerned to find suitable partners for the younger generation.) However, the pressure on girls is much greater as they have only a few chances of someone asking for their hand. By contrast, men are free to request a woman's hand in marriage at any time and as often as they like, so for them there is no question of 'missing the boat'.

Writing on the family, Nahas has explained the main reasons behind the encouragement of marriage in the Arab world. He notes that while Islam urges people to marry, the social climate of most Arab countries arouses sexual impulses early, although tradition still enforces sexual segregation. The marriage of girls also relieves the family of worry about their virginity. Finally, the desire for children is very strong among the Arabs. Older people within the family are proud of having grandchildren, due to 'the tribal spirit of most of the Arab people'.[1] For all these reasons very few women in the Arab world stay unmarried.

Traditional and Contemporary Marriages

In the Arab world, marriage is traditionally a joining of two families, rather than of two individuals. Couples in the West tend to go through the phases of meeting, starting to like each other, friendship, dating, courtship, then engagement. Each of these phases, particularly the last two, can take many months or years before the actual day of the wedding. The traditional Arab marriage, on the other hand, starts and ends with one stage: the official wedding day. In this case, couples are not even allowed to see each other before the wedding day, although the practice is contrary to Islam.

Traditionally, when a man asks for a girl's hand in marriage, her family is expected to delay the answer, especially if they wish to accept him. If they plan to refuse him, they will give him an excuse as soon as possible; otherwise they will keep delaying. Such a delay is considered to display the high esteem in which the family hold their daughter. A quick decision might imply that they were eager to rid themselves of her, and the family of the bridegroom would value her less if they accepted right away. Given this tradition, the bridegroom's family visit and send messages at least once a week in order to gain the agreement of the bride's family. There is another reason behind this custom, however: if a complete stranger were to ask for a girl's hand in marriage, her family would need time to make inquiries about him and his family background in order to be sure he came from an honourable family. The bride's family openly defends this action and gives it as a reason for the delay.

Apart from those who married relatives, the majority of the women I interviewed indicated that they had agreed to a proposal of marriage at least two months after it was originally requested. One woman, Muna, complained about her husband and related his behaviour to his poor background, saying that if she had married a man from a background similar to hers he would not behave like that. When I asked why her family had not made inquiries first, she said they lived far away and the only way they could get information was to ask a relative who worked in the Ministry of Education to look up his personal file–her husband was a teacher. This file had revealed positive information.

Marriage is arranged when the bridegroom's family wants. An adult male has no right to express his wish to get married; it is up to the family to decide when their son is to marry and whom he marries. Adult daughters are not allowed to tell their parents whom they wish to marry, or to choose their husbands.[2]

The fact that a man can ask for a girl's hand in marriage but not the other way round leads to increased anxiety on the part of the girl's parents. Hence they make more attempts to control her and pressure her into acceptance than they might make in relation to a boy, and the pressure increases with her age. In these circumstances, girls have no choice but to wait for someone to propose to them. Sometimes the family is considering more than one offer at the same time. If all the men who propose are strangers, most girls choose the richest, the man who can provide the best house (separate from his parents) and the best furniture; they will also opt for the more educated man, from a better family, and perhaps one with a pleasant appearance too. This applied particularly in the past when only the family were concerned with the choice but it still applies today, when girls have more say in selecting one of their suitors.[3]

At the formal engagement, the groom gives the bride a gift (usually a watch, ring, necklace or bracelet) as well as the wedding ring. The value and numbers of such items reflect the status of the bridegroom's family, their wealth and their evaluation of the bride. For example, if they very much wanted the marriage to take place and struggled to gain acceptance from the bride's family, they might borrow money to buy a better gift for the bride even if they are poor.

Marriages nowadays fall into two main categories: arranged (ranging from the strict traditional marriage to one that is still arranged but less strict) and contemporary. In the strict traditional marriage, all the arrangements fall on the families. The couple only see each other once or twice before the wedding, and then only in the company of the families. A less strict arranged marriage would still be agreed on by the families, but the couple might see each other several times before the wedding, always with a chaperone at home. In the least strict form of arranged marriage the family might arrange a party at which the couple could meet. Courtship would then take place but always under surveillance even if the couple went out together.

Muslims may not go out together after the engagement; they have to wait until after the wedding ceremony and the signing of the contract. There is still a period after the wedding before the marriage is consummated–this might take anything from a few days to a year or two, and during this time the couple may go out together without a chaperone. When the marriage is finally consummated the couple might have their honeymoon and move in together, when of course there are no more restrictions.

The following are two cases representing the strict traditional arranged marriage in which the bride does not see her husband until the official wedding or engagement day:

I didn't know him beforehand. When they brought the engagement ring, they told me to come and sit with him. I was afraid, and he thought I didn't want him. I didn't know what was going on. He asked my father why he hadn't given me some idea of what was happening. My father said that I was still very young and he should teach me what to do after marriage. Later on, my mother and my aunts began to explain what marriage was all about. They said I should feel happy. (*Majida*)

It was an arranged marriage. When I saw him at the registry office and discovered he was bald and ugly, I told my sister I didn't want to marry him. On the celebration on the seventh day of my marriage, an army major sent his family to ask for my hand. He didn't know that I was already married. I felt sad and thought how unlucky I was. Why did he have to come so late? (*Nazhat*)

This marriage tradition still exists in most parts of the Arab world and has changed little from the old customs. A great many marriages still take place between two people who hardly know each other. Contemporary marriage is different; in most cases, the couple meet beforehand and may even know each other as a result of working in the same office, for example. But meetings prior to marriage are still supposed to take place with other members of the family present.

The engagement is quickly followed by the signing of the marriage contract, which states what the bridegroom must give to the bride. The *mahar* is the money, gold and material possessions given to the bride in two parts, one paid in advance, the other at a later stage of marriage, whether or not it ends in divorce. If a man wishes to divorce his wife and the second part of the *mahar* is paid, the divorce is considered absolute. The bride's family is normally most concerned with the second sum of the *mahar*, since a large sum is presumed to constitute a deterrent to divorce.

The official ceremony of the signing of the contract used to be the actual marriage day. Nowadays, this is not usually the case and people try to arrange to sign the contract soon after the engagement, as only then will the couple be free to see each other, with or without the presence of other members of the family, since they are officially considered husband and wife.

After the signing of the contract, the consummation of the marriage may be delayed for many months until the couple have made preparations, found a flat, and so on. Girls do not go out with their fiances after the engagement, but after the signing of the contract. The contract is a commitment in writing, and if the bridegroom thereafter wishes to leave the girl, he must pay both the first and second parts of the *mahar* since this would be considered a divorce. If the couple can prove that they did not have sexual intercourse during the time between the wedding ceremony and their actually living together, then the bridegroom need pay only half the money.

Nowadays, although the same formalities regarding the engagement and wedding contract survive, the *mahar* is not often paid in cash, as it used to be. The trend is towards spending the money on such material possessions as furniture for the couple. Bahira and Nada both experienced the less strict form of an arranged marriage:

He's related to me and I was known to his family from a very early age. Then when I grew up, they asked for my hand. I was 12 when they came to ask about me. My family also asked some questions about the man who wanted to marry me. He wanted to see me and at first my family refused. Then they consented to his visiting me. Of course, his friends urged him to meet me to find out if I was OK and not blind or lame, as he later told me. After meeting me, he approved of me, and a month later we got married. (*Bahira*)

It was an arranged marriage, but I asked to talk to him on more than one occasion, when I was able to put forward all my views and find out what his were, get to know him a bit more . . . and I think this was a successful arrangement. (*Nada*)

The changes within society generally have affected the system of arranged marriage, so it has become less strict than it used to be. Such changes are comparatively new developments, but the arranged marriage is slowly, though surely, disappearing. More precisely, it is being eased out; it is not the whole of the custom which is disappearing, but rather the way in which it takes place.[4]

The majority of the women I talked to appeared to be in arranged marriages, whether strict or non-strict, irrespective of their background and educational level. The changes which have occurred within the system of arranged marriage cannot be labelled clearly or identified as belonging to particular classes. In fact, different forms of marriage may take place within one family. For example, if a girl is not educated or does not have a paid job, it would be difficult for her to meet a prospective husband. There would be no other suitable meeting-place, and even if the family were not very traditional, such couples would only meet after talks concerning their marriage had already started.

Marriage between Cousins

In Iraqi society it is very common for cousins to marry. The most favoured cousins are the sons and daughters of the father's brothers, since the father's family is considered to be more important than that of the mother. Even among the father's family, his brothers' sons are more important than his sisters'. In general, whether cousins or just close relatives, such marriages are greatly preferred to marriages to strangers, despite the fact that the former are not encouraged by Islam.[5]

In the past, a paternal cousin could prevent the marriage of his female cousin to someone else, if he so wished. The custom was called *nahua*. Furthermore, he had the same authority over the girl as that of her own brother or father. These practices still exist in rural Iraq, and in some urban areas also. Several of the women I interviewed had married a cousin:

A cousin asked for my hand, but he had problems with my father and was rejected. Another cousin heard about it and came asking for my hand. My father agreed. As you know, a girl can't say no to her father. I didn't want to marry, but it is written. (*Amal*)

Strict arranged marriages were common in Iraq up to the early 1950s. In fact, it was virtually unheard of for couples to see each other before marriage in the 1940s, unless they were cousins. This is despite the fact that Islam allows the couple not only to meet before marriage but also to eat together and talk to each other, and so determine their suitability, as long as they keep within the bounds of religion and morality. However, this rule of Islam was not practised, unless the couple were cousins. It is in men's interest not to allow women much choice as to their partners. The patriarchal system in Iraq is so strong that it has survived changes which were introduced by Islam.

Love and Marriage

It is commonly believed that love between partners arises after marriage, whether or not the marriage has been arranged. Furthermore, many women deny that their marriage was arranged, saying that there was some kind of a relationship beforehand. I was interested to learn about the nature of this relationship. I asked the women I interviewed, 'Did you marry for love? If not, how was your marriage arranged and how do you feel about it?' As described above, virtually all were in arranged marriages of some kind, so their reactions to the concept of marrying for love must be put into context.

The word 'love' is not viewed with favour in Iraqi society, and its utterance is sometimes forbidden. The girl who falls in love brings shame on her family. In the distant past and up to the 1940s, if a man loved a girl and this relationship became known publicly, the girl's family would never agree to marry her to him, as this might seem to be public acknowledgement of their love affair. However, love affairs still bring great unrest and anxiety to the family. Many of the women mentioned, in one way or another, that they did not believe love marriages were happier than arranged marriages. This may be because of the connection between love and dishonour for girls. However, the reason behind women's resistance to modernization, which aims to abolish the arranged marriage and replace it with a love match, is the increasing incidence of men merely using girls. Through such affairs women believe they lose not only their reputation but also the man himself, since he would prefer to marry someone who had never loved a man before. Thus he would start looking, or rather, allow his family to arrange for his marriage with another woman. Most men believe that if a girl loves him, she is not honourable and might love someone else. The following quotations show this:

I haven't experienced love. Love before marriage proves to be a failure, because if either partner suspected the other, they would say, 'You could have loved someone else.' (*Siham*)

No, I don't think that marriages for love are successful. Sometimes love creates problems. Nowadays this generation love each other, but a boy would most probably leave his girlfriend and then she would be jilted. (*Jumana*)[6]

Iraqi men may show loving behaviour to girls, perhaps imitating what they have seen on television or films. The cinema has taught women that Western men open car doors for them, stand up when they walk in, help them on with their coats, buy them presents and, more important, treat them as loving companions in the home, rather than as servants. But Arab men have not learned the Western habits which accompany such behaviour, that is, they do not then wish to marry the girl they love.[7]

The same attitude is found in Egypt,[8] where a study found that a large percentage of women still wish to marry in the traditional way. One of the women is quoted as saying:

> Although I want to marry someone I like . . . I still need my family's opinion . . . they want my own good . . . Men have many faces, and due to my limited experience I need my family's help to see them all . . . If the family take the responsibility, they will bear the consequences.

Many of the women I spoke to expressed similar feelings. Nor do these views differ much among university students, as shown by research on love and marriage among Iraqi students at the University of Mosul.[9] Most male students were in favour of love affairs between students, while female students had different views. Here are some typical answers:

> I agree that love affairs exist within the university campus, but 95% are doomed to failure. They only last while students are doing their studies. It's like a hobby. A male student would never choose his girlfriend as a wife to share his life.

Another female student said:

> Yes, there are love affairs but all of them have negative aspects and are bound to fail because they are built on false hopes and groundless promises.

In other words, the girls do not think a love relationship with a man will lead to marriage—marriage being the ultimate goal. Of all the women I interviewed, there was only one case in which a woman had loved her husband and had a 'limited' relationship with him for over three years before they married.

A few women said that they had married for love; they had either married a cousin or got to know their husband very briefly before marriage, although the type of relationship they had did not appear to allow them to get to know their partner well. Fatima provides a good example of this kind of relationship:

I used to believe in love but now I don't know what I believe. My marriage is not successful despite the fact that it is based on love, so I don't know what is right. Men hide their real personality during engagement, or while they are in love, but later on, their true faces come to the surface, which is a totally different thing.

The point raised by Fatima–that men hide their real personalities–was expressed frequently by many other women, chiefly in discussing the engagement period, and how they did not know their husbands particularly well, despite having met several times and going out together. They explained that love affairs were not the answer, since men tend to hide their real personalities, often appearing affectionate, understanding and kind.

This issue was also raised when the women were asked whether they preferred female or male bosses. Because they were not comparing the man's attitude before and after marriage, and because their relationship with a boss differs from that with a husband, none of the women considered that male bosses concealed a different personality. Indeed, they said that men were more kind and understanding as bosses. So it appears that men do indeed have different behaviour patterns towards the people in their lives, according to whether the situation is public or private.

Girls' Expectations of Future Husbands

Although the family's role in choosing partners for their children is less important than it used to be, there is still a strong social prejudice against a love match. This prejudice is often justified by reference to the high divorce rate in the West. If love relationships are a good way of choosing the right partner, people ask, why does the divorce rate in the West remain the highest in the world?

In recent years many young people in Iraq have begun going out together even if they are not married. Their parents rarely know or approve, so their meetings take place in an unnatural atmosphere. This creates great unrest and fear and does not allow them to get to know each other well. Most love relationships occur between students at university, but they do not tend to end in marriage for a number of reasons, one of which may be their similarity in age. Both partners start work or a career at the same time, and since marriage is very expensive, it is not practically possible for at least six years after graduation. In the meantime, girls face great pressure from the family and society to accept other proposals, and most do so. According to the women I spoke to, prior knowledge of a future husband's personal character is an important issue. Such information cannot be gained through asking about the man as part of the arranged marriage procedure, nor can it be known from a short period of seeing each other. This is a major problem in the marriage system.

In order to gain further information on this point, I asked the following questions: 'Did you place any conditions on your acceptance of marriage? If so, what were they?'

> I wanted him to have a strong personality, to be outspoken and to be able to express his feelings towards me. I wanted him to have fair views about women, as some men regard women with contempt. (*Ibtihal*)

It was important for me to marry someone who was natural. I
like a happy, outgoing man, not one who complicates things,
but of course I didn't get all that I wanted. (*Samar*)

Many women answered the question by criticizing their husbands:

The most important conditions I had were that he shouldn't
drink, should behave reasonably well in public and think before
he spoke. I didn't mind what he looked like or what he owned.
It was important for me that he was successful at work and had
a good reputation, and was tied to a timetable, as I didn't trust
men outside their homes. None of the above came true. I still
believe these were appropriate conditions to hope for, because
they would be a relief to me and grant me what I want. (*Fadwa*)

Fadwa wanted her husband to be 'tied to a timetable' because
she 'didn't trust men outside their homes'. I then asked about her
family, and learned that her parents and her brothers all worked
in jobs which tied them to a timetable. This represented her ideal
because, as the saying goes, *kullo fataten be abeha muajaba* (Every girl
admires her father). I should point out that Fadwa's feeling that
men are not trustworthy is shared by most women, but the idea of
tying them to a definite schedule–in other words, controlling
them–is new for a woman. From this, I suspect that Fadwa had not
thought of this prior to marriage but discovered it in retrospect as
something she wished she had known.

Ahlam reflected another idea:

Money didn't matter to me. I wanted a man who respected a
woman as a woman and as a human being and who had good
manners.

Ahlam emphasized 'good manners' (also mentioned by many of

the other women), but she associated this with the desire to be respected by her husband. By getting married, girls dream of a better life with a well-mannered man, and their aspirations stop here.

Another woman, who did not have clear ideas or conditions about the acceptance of marriage, said:

> I wish I'd married a sincere man and heard a nice word from him. I wanted him to be truthful and have a good attitude and manners towards me. Of course, I feel these things now, but before marriage I had no conditions as I didn't think about marriage or want to get married. However, even if I did, I wouldn't have been able to find out such information about him, despite the fact that he's a relative of mine. (*Amina*)

This important issue concerns every woman, whether she discovers the importance of such things before or after her marriage. It is difficult for a woman to discover her husband's character without knowing him well. As a relative, Amina would have been allowed to mix with her prospective husband to a certain extent, but that would never have allowed her the opportunity to discover such important things as his daily behaviour, his ideas, attitudes, and so on. In any case, unmarried girls cannot learn very much about men through their own fathers and brothers (who are the only men they have known in their lives so far), as such experience differs greatly from life with a partner.

Fatima's story illustrates her disappointment at not achieving what she had hoped for in her future husband. It also indicates the basic requirements girls aim for in a husband:

> Like most girls, I had a basic condition. I wanted him to be rich, since I'm used to spending lavishly. I wanted a man with good status and a good family and who was open-minded. When I

got married none of my wishes came true. On the contrary, I went backwards. On the other hand, he is happy. He got all he wanted. He has a home, a wife, food ready and clean clothes.

Women are brought up to believe in the ideal of a strong man, who controls women in every way. As Ansam explained:

To have a good appearance is desirable, but to me the most important thing is for a man to have high moral standards and a strong personality, to be in control, as I do not like a man to be controlled by a woman . . . I mean, he does not let his woman behave as she pleases, go out, quarrel about trivial matters, and her word is not the one that goes at home.

Ansam is educated and has a paid job, which implies that there must be things in everyday life which she might disagree about and that she should have some freedom to do things her own way. Despite this, she strongly supported the traditional notion of masculine superiority because women are socialized to believe that a strong dominant man is the ideal.

Although many of the women denied it, material possessions and wealth were also important to them. The question arises, however, as to what are material concerns. If education is measured only by certificates, is wanting an educated husband not a material condition? Nada told me:

I had no material conditions. I wanted him to be of at least the same academic level as I am because there were complications between my father and mother due to their different intellectual levels, and that was the cause of their divorce.

She also questioned recent social changes which have given women the freedom to accept or reject proposals, yet denied them the opportunity to judge a man's character by getting to know him well. Many women expressed a wish to marry non-materialistic husbands who would love and cherish them, and so on. But because the present system of marriage makes it almost impossible to discover such things in advance, they accepted the *status quo*. In general, girls are brought up to believe that it is immoral to attach great importance to material things or to stress this when choosing a husband. In practice, however, they find themselves forced to choose on a materialistic basis since there are no other grounds for choice.

Most of the women's expectations of their husband were related to character, attitudes and ways of thinking. As they confirmed, such personal attributes are very difficult to discover beforehand unless the woman forms a close, long-term relationship with the man. Thus a girl can only evaluate her prospective husband in terms of 'materialistic conditions'. Several women mentioned in one way or another that they did not care for material things. Others indicated that they did not think about stipulating conditions. They gave reasons such as the fact that they were not in a position to choose, since their marriage had been arranged for them since infancy, or that 'good girls' should not think about marriage in trying to fit into the social ideal of feminine behaviour. For example, Sahira said:

> We didn't know any of these things and they didn't cross our mind. We used to say that it was up to our parents to decide about our marriage.

Fate and Destiny
Whether the preferences women mention are ideal or practical, whether they still think that their conditions are important or whether they are satisfied with their marriages, most women in Iraq (and in other Middle Eastern societies) believe in fate and

destiny. They are all taught to accept their marriages, whatever they bring, and to rationalize their acceptance as *maktub*, 'It is written.' They are taught that everyone has a fate which never changes: 'Who knows? If I'd married another man it could have been even worse,' is a common statement. Several of the women I spoke to, after indicating that their choice of husband was not a good one, concluded, 'It is written,' or 'It is our fate.'

Why Women Marry

Throughout the Middle East, there are very few single women over the age of 30. The absence of non-legalized co-habitation and illegitimacy shows how little intimate interaction there is between the sexes.[10] Whatever her social situation, by a certain age a girl is expected to be married. Girls are brought up to believe in the importance of marriage, and great pressure is put on them to marry. This frequently leads them to believe that marriage is inevitable, and that they must accept a proposal as soon as possible, bearing in mind that their first chances are the best. As they grow older they lose their beauty, and the quality of the proposals will drop; they reach a point when they are likely to agree to any proposal that comes along, especially if pressure is applied or there is also encouragement from the family.

In Iraq, the age of marriage differs from one social category to another. For example, some of the teachers I spoke to were as old as 26 when they married. The age among the higher professionals rose even higher to 35, but it dropped to 12 with the housewives. (Although only a few of the housewives had married at the age of 12, the majority of them were married by the time they were 16 or 17.) Almost half of the women indicated that they had married mainly to satisfy their parents or their mothers:

I rejected the men who came forward to ask for my hand. My mother felt awful about this. She even used to sit and cry.

Father also felt hurt. So I felt I must get married, and I accepted my present husband without knowing anything about him. Anyway, a woman at a marriageable age needs a man to complete her life. Without a man her life isn't complete. (*Hala*)

Status is one reason for the parents' intense pressure on girls to marry, as an unmarried daughter would reflect badly on them. Feryal's mother's attitude is typical, but it is unusual for the father not to feel the same, unless he has misgivings about the bridegroom:

Mother was the reason. She used to say that I was grown up; why was I still not married? Father was proud of me and wanted me to stay at home longer, but she used to say to him, 'What will people say: we don't want to marry her off because of the income she brings us?' (*Feryal*)

The second most important reason the women gave for getting married was to gain a better status for themselves, and to feel freer:

I got married mainly to satisfy my parents. Also they taught me about marriage, so I thought I'd become an important part of a household, where I could go out as I pleased. But later I realized that I'd become even more restricted. (*Amina*)

I thought marriage would give me an identity. (*Fadwa*)

I expected married life to be different and more fun, not like still being a girl where society looks at what I wear and what I say. I thought, 'I'll be freer.' Marriage is inevitable in this society. One cannot stay unmarried. My cousin wanted to marry me and I had a number of proposals from other men, so I just wanted to get married to finish with it and to have peace of mind. (*Fatima*)

Other women said they had married in order to stop people asking why they were still single:

I knew that people wondered why I wasn't married, even if they didn't always say it. (*Suha*)

The most important reason for accepting is to stop people from asking why you are still single, which led to pressure from my family on me to get married. Before my marriage, I was like an uncrowned queen compared to the way I am now. (*Suhad*)

Other women spoke of the 'right marriage age', which is a form of parental pressure, derived from social pressure.

In addition, many thought that marriage would be fun and that they would be freer and more important:

I thought it would be fun. I didn't know what it was all about. (*Bahira*)

What is interesting is that every girl is taught to believe that marriage brings happiness, rather than responsibilities. They appear to learn this attitude from socialization rather than from reality–the kinds of lives led by mothers and wives around them do not appear to influence this belief very much. Apparently they feel that the unhappy marriages they see around them are exceptions to the general rule they have been taught. So they struggle to achieve an ideal which in reality is unattainable, and when they do not achieve it they feel unhappy and guilty.

One woman pointed to a factor which could apply to many

others–the fear of living under the control of a sister- or brother-in-law:

> I got married maybe due to all the reasons you mention, and perhaps not to be at the mercy of my sister- or brother-in-law if I stayed unmarried, since I wouldn't have been allowed to live on my own. (*Fadwa*)

This fear arises out of the social control of women, who are not allowed to live alone apart from their family. So when the parents die, a woman whose brothers and sisters were all married might have to live with one of them, or keep moving from one to another until she reached her late 40s. Then she would no longer be wanted by men, which might result in some extra social respect for her, allowing her to live on her own. Sometimes this looks like a good reason to enter into a marriage, or to remain within an unhappy one, because to suffer from a husband seems easier than to suffer from one's own family. A husband is only one person, but if a woman's family were to trouble her, there would be a lot of them.[11]

Some of the interviewees experienced cruelty in their own families and chose marriage as a solution, like running away from home. Rafida is a good example:

> I was 6 years old when I used to visit our next-door neighbour who has seven daughters, all older than me, who used to love me very much, and praise my dress and appearance. I used to enjoy going there very much. One day I forgot to tell anyone at home that I was going there, and I had so much fun that I stayed for four hours. When I returned my older sister was furious. She shouted at me for not telling them where I was. They were looking all over for me. Next I was held down by my two brothers while my sister heated a metal poker in the fire. She

burned my leg, telling me that this would be a lesson I would never forget.

In Rafida's case there was no question of the family being poor, or the child being extremely badly behaved, or in some way unacceptable through deformity, for example. Even if this were the case, such behaviour by the older sister would not be tolerable. In Rafida's case the cruelty was based on attitude. This example shows to what lengths the family will go to protect its honour, as punishment will make the girl think twice about going somewhere without the family's agreement. In such circumstances married life seems preferable to all other alternatives:

I felt so happy. I thought: once and for all, I will free myself from my parents. (*Labiba*)

I wanted to settle down by getting married and building my own family, and leaving home where I felt oppressed. These are two main reasons, and probably also because I was past the usual age of marriage. (*Hajir*)

When a man has financial problems, or if he or his family think there might be problems with his wife due to his behaviour or attitudes, the family may prefer to find a submissive wife for him. Such a wife would prefer to suffer with him rather than go back to her family as women normally do when they have problems with their husbands. Such marriages are considered happy, despite the difficulties both husband and wife experience, because the wife tries to make the best of things for herself and her husband. She has no alternative, either being unwanted by her family or not wishing to return to them.

In conclusion, it can be seen that marriage is almost obligatory for young Iraqi women. Social control operates by putting pressure on them through the family and society to the extent that they see it as their only future. Although factors such as education and jobs for women are giving them more choice among suitors, the importance of moral values, family origins and reputation remains very great.[12]

3
Worlds Apart: Sexual Life for Women and Men

Attitudes towards Sex

Q: How well would you say you and your husband get on, in general?

A: The most important things for him are food and sex. When we first married, I had such a rough time living with his sister. I couldn't wear make-up or dress up the way I like, as she gets jealous. He used to say to me, 'Stop wearing make-up, don't do this, don't wear that. What are you trying to do? She gets hurt.' When she got married, that was one problem out of the way.

Q: Is your husband an affectionate person? Does he express it? In what way?

A: A wife needs sympathy and understanding, but he hardly says a nice word to me. Sometimes I ask him whether he loves me and he says, 'If I didn't, I wouldn't buy you and your children all that you need.' I say, 'But a woman likes to hear a nice word from her husband.' He replies, 'Women who hear soft talk misbehave.' I'm telling you, if he smiled once I'd say, 'The sun's come out.'

Q: What about his anger? Does he express it? In what way?

A: He has a loud mouth. He always shouts at me and threatens me with divorce. He demands my approval for everything he does.

Q: What about the sexual side of things? Have you had any difficulties or problems with this?

A: Whenever he wants me, I'm ready. If he goes to the bedroom, even if he doesn't call me, I go to him and ask if he wants me. Sometimes he says yes; others no, he's tired. I think I must fear God. I believe that if women don't obey men, particularly in such matters, God, the heavens and the holy spirits will never bless them.

Q: What about you? Do you think sex is important for women too?

A: Well, he doesn't really care much whether I do or not. Sometimes I even try to mention it to him indirectly, but he doesn't pay any attention. You know, I'm very good to him. He doesn't like me to go out, so I don't. I obey all his orders. I take good care of him, but he doesn't take care of me. Sometimes I get angry. Once, I decided to say 'no' to him. He said, 'What about God and the holy spirits? Don't you fear them?'

Q: So it was he who taught you that?

A: No, I already believed it. It was my mother, God bless her soul, who taught me that and I told him about it. (*Majida*)

I have quoted Majida's answers at length because they may be seen as representative of the experience of many Iraqi women. From what she and other women told me, it is obvious that the relationship between husbands and wives in Iraq remains, as it has traditionally been, based on power. Husbands expect to command their wives rather than love them. Even when they care about their wives the social system does not allow them to show it, so the wives are unaware of their husbands' feelings. It is believed that there is a fundamental biological difference between men and women: sexual satisfaction is seen as a 'need' for men and as a 'service' for women. Thus women's nature is believed to be receptive and frigid, while men have strong sexual desires and are active in the sexual act. Girls are socialized to regard sex as predominantly a male concern; they are brought up to avoid any behaviour defined as sexual, such as dressing in a particular way, laughing or even walking freely, because an 'honourable' girl ought not to do anything which might lead men to desire her.

Young females are socialized to fear men and sexuality and to protect their virginity at all costs. They are taught to avoid strenuous exercise, jumping from heights, or sitting on sharp edges, in order to keep their hymen intact. Correspondingly, the parents' most important duty is to ensure their daughter remains a virgin until her wedding day. This part of a girl's body is considered to be more important even than her eyes, arms or lower limbs.[1]

The majority of young women enter marriage in a state of almost complete sexual ignorance, which is seen as a sign of honour.[2] Young women are expected to be pure and virginal in mind and body, or to be frigid: this makes their exploitation complete and absolute. The women I interviewed described experiences that derive from this social conditioning:

I remember that from a very early age I was afraid of men. I used to hear a lot of stories–about this woman whose life was ruined because she was raped, and another girl who got pregnant and her family killed her . . . and so on. I was so terrified that when I went to buy material for a dress and the salesman touched my hand, I felt as if I'd committed a crime. (*Jumana*)

One of my friends told me about how a woman gets pregnant. She told me that this could happen starting at the age of 10, which worried me. I was even more worried when my mother told me at the age of 12 not to sit on the bath seat [a small wooden seat] when taking a bath after my father or my brother unless I washed it very thoroughly with hot water. She also told me not to mix my clothes with theirs on the same washing line on the roof, for fear I might get pregnant. The idea gave me lots of worries and nightmares. (*Fadwa*)

On the other hand many men, particularly in urban areas, have some sexual experience before marriage. This is accepted by society, though it tends to be limited experience and gained mainly with prostitutes. Both sexes consider pre-marital sexual experience for men to be an advantage. The lack of such experience may be seen as a reason for unsuccessful marital relations and even the breakdown of the marriage. Nazira illustrates this point of view:

He doesn't know much about how to treat a woman, maybe because of the kind of life he led before marriage. He'd never been with a woman before. No experience at all.

From my observations and from the answers given to me, it seems that social traditions which derive from bedouin roots are still so strong that education and social class have little bearing on men's attitudes towards women and sexuality. Samar's words support this view:

He got his higher degree from the US; he's quite sophisticated. Of course, he knows all about women and sex, but a degree doesn't always make much difference, it's more important how you're brought up. Don't you agree?

Sexual experience for women, on the other hand, is generally considered to be a disadvantage, even if 'legitimately' gained in a previous marriage. In the marriage market, a female who is a virgin is more desirable than one who is not.[3] Men tend to leave a woman they love if she consents to a sexual relationship of any kind, regarding her as 'loose' and dishonourable, and certainly not to be trusted as a wife.

Because females are so thoroughly socialized to fear sexual relations, the honeymoon, while pleasurable for the man, is invariably the worst period of marital life for the woman. As discussed earlier, limited and often inaccurate sexual knowledge provides the woman with false ideas of sexuality. She carries this fear to her wedding day, making it a day of dread. In order to counteract this fear and to determine whether their hymen was intact, most of the women I interviewed took medical advice before their marriage, in case they had lost their virginity by accident–if they were no longer virgins, they might not have gone through with the marriage.

Despite these precautions, the fear is easing slightly nowadays. The old custom of showing a blood-stained sheet on the wedding night, to prove the bride's virginity, has now almost vanished among middle-class urban Iraqis. Another fast-disappearing traditional practice is the bridegroom's slaughtering a cat as the bride enters the bridal chamber before they have sexual intercourse. This was done to scare the bride into obedience, based on the belief that if she were to disobey the husband's demand for sex on the first night of marriage, it might make him permanently impotent. Even among the urban poor, this custom is fast disappearing.

For some of the women I spoke to, their first experience of sex can only be described as traumatic:

I started to fear men the first day I was married. He attacked me all of a sudden. I saw him forcing me. He was like a wolf. It was a nightmare. Some men start by talking to the woman, trying to make it easier for her, but he didn't. (*Fawzia*)

He raped me in the train on our wedding day. I was 13 years old. I'd met him face to face for the first time that day; we were on the way to our honeymoon in Basra. I started screaming as I was so scared, but I stopped when he started hitting me. I remember very well now that all I wanted then was my mother. I felt that I was with a stranger who was harming me badly. After he finished having sex with me he left me alone, but I felt it was the end of the world for me; everything seemed ugly and those children who I used to play with seemed so far away and I was so alienated. (*Zahra*)

Sex and Knowledge

Although women have very limited knowledge of sex before marriage, I was interested in discovering where such knowledge came from. The following comment is fairly typical:

My information about sex began during my adolescence and came through my friends at school. That information was very limited, and wasn't at all applicable to the real situation I came to know after marriage. (*Zainab*)

Ignorance on the part of both women and men can make sex a problem. Even when partners become sexually experienced, as sometimes happens after long years of marriage, they may still feel insecure regarding their own sexuality. Many women are unaware that a female orgasm exists. They try not to admit that they need satisfaction or to mention such needs even to their husbands 'to keep their dignity' (see the comments by Ansam at the end of this chapter). Thus women experience a conflict at this level, which can develop into considerable unhappiness within marriage.

Iraqi men tend to have minimal knowledge of female anatomy, and they either do not know how to or do not wish to arouse their wives.[4] Most of the interviewees said that they experienced no physical contact as such during intercourse, apart from genital contact. Despite this lack of physical intimacy several women indicated that their husband had a very strong sex drive:

Sex is the most important thing to my husband. It may be the only thing in life that's important to him. He always wants me to dress up in my sexiest nightgown and respond happily and willingly to all his desires. But look at me; I come home from work very tired. At home, the children and the housework make me even more tired, so I don't feel like wearing make-up every evening and doing what he wants, because I'm exhausted. I'd like to talk to someone about my problems, but he doesn't listen to me because he thinks it doesn't concern him. When I don't get changed and dress the way he wants me to, I feel as if I'm punishing him for what he's doing to me. I know this is wrong, but to tell you the truth, I don't care much about sex. I don't know why. (*Suha*)

Suha's experience highlights the fundamental paradox. Men's expectations of sex are high, but since women have no experience and their husbands have no interest in making it pleasurable, it is hard for them to achieve sexual satisfaction. It is important to stress that the men themselves do not wish to initiate their wives into sexual fulfilment because they believe it will make them promiscuous.[5] Furthermore, they treat their wives as possessions and take them for granted–this is in strict contrast to the period before marriage, when they try to be seen as considerate and charming.

Fatima was the only woman I spoke to who had married for love and been friends with her husband for three years beforehand. Nevertheless:

> In the engagement period, we used to go out for meals and he used to give me a lot of presents. Then after our marriage, he stopped doing that and I realized he was mean. Only then did I realize he's not romantic and is very limited in the way he expresses his love to me.

Her husband's attitude changed with marriage: he no longer had to be considerate or say nice words to her, because marriage was the end of the matter. He knew his wife could not afford to leave him because she had become 'used' and would not be able to get another man with his 'good qualities'. For a man, probably the most important reason to marry is sex.[6] It is interesting to consider Fatima's reply to my question, 'What about the sexual side of things?':

> In this area, he's all right. At school sometimes, I hear other teachers talking about the way their husbands attack them like wolves when they demand sex. I would say mine is not like that at all.

All the women's answers confirmed how paradoxical sexuality is for Iraqi couples. For women the dilemma is particularly acute. Women are brought up to believe that sex is filthy, shameful and sinful; however, sex is their duty in which they should fulfil the husband's needs. Yet if it is sinful, why did God instruct people to practise it? A woman must please her husband, yet remain chaste and demure. This leads us to the issue of sex and duty.

Sex and Duty

Iraqi women are taught to believe that to treat their husband well in bed, that is, to obey demands for sexual intercourse, fulfils their duty to God. Because of this, they put up with their husband's bad behaviour, and try to please him just the same. Khadija's response illustrates this point:

> When he wants it, he gets it and right afterwards, he treats me like a pig. I never cared about sex, and when somebody scares you 24 hours a day and swears about your mother and father, how would you see him? Plus he always gives orders. He doesn't ask for it in a nice way, but, again, I tend to say, 'It's my duty. God will not bless me if I don't do it.'

Interestingly, while both Khadija (above) and Majida (at the beginning of this chapter) regarded sex as 'fulfilling their duty to God', they were otherwise not religious. Majida showed clearly that her husband was using her belief to dominate her.

Girls are also taught from an early age that men in general are unfaithful and not to be trusted. By keeping a watchful eye on her husband, treating him well and trying to please him, particularly in bed, a wife will ensure that he remains faithful to her.[7] Despite being subjected to ill-treatment, women cite numerous reasons for complying with their husband's demands for sexual intercourse. But the key factor which emerged from the interviews is the deep-rooted belief that women are 'naturally' subservient to men. So totally indoctrinated are they with this ideology that they fear that any attempt to overthrow it would result in 'justifiable' violence. Here are some of the women's answers to my questions:

> For him, a woman's place is in the home, taking care of her husband and children and doing the housework; she shouldn't

complain or object to anything. She should be ready for her husband with her best make-up on before going to bed. She ought to drop everything if he asks her to come to bed.

Q: Do you do what you said, wear make-up and so on for him before going to bed?

A: You know, even if I were very busy, he would demand it of me, and if I refused, he'd make a scene.

Q: What about you? Do you think sex is important for women too?

A: It isn't important to me. I don't care much about it. I almost always allow him to have sex with me but, to tell you the truth, I really wish he wouldn't touch me. But I don't let him know that because, once when I did tell him, we had a big fight. He told me that even if we'd had a big fight and he'd beat me, I should still say yes to sex with him afterwards if he asked for it, that I am a woman and ought to obey him. 'Why have I married you?' he asks. You know, I sometimes think of a solution. I think, what if I pretend I want him and that I enjoy sex? Then I change my mind. Knowing him, even if I could keep pretending forever, which is difficult enough, it wouldn't solve the problem. He's a very jealous man; he'd accuse me of having affairs then. (*Muna*)

He takes but he never gives. Sometimes, when I don't feel in the mood, he forces me, saying it's his right. I say, 'All right, but you shouldn't order me around like that.' If someone is upset or has problems, why should they always have to be willing? He will say, 'But I work away; when I come home, I demand my rights.' Well, what can I do? I usually say it's all right. I know if I don't, he'll be very angry and he might spend the following day screaming at everyone.

Q: What about you? Do you think sex is important to you?

A: Not really. I don't like any of his behaviour towards me.

And I'm always tired, I work both inside and outside the home. How do you expect me to respond to him? (*Shada*)

Like Muna and Shada, most of the women saw sex as an exclusively male concern. Thus they tended to see it as a duty:

Well, yes, some women enjoy sex, but they're exceptional. Most women don't. They just don't attach much importance to such matters. (*Zainab*)

No, women don't care much for these things. I don't believe any woman cares about sex. Women are different from men, you know what I mean? (*Zahida*)

I can't speak for others, but myself, I don't care about it at all. (*Sahira*)

The following passages clearly indicate that sex is a duty. There was no foreplay during sexual intercourse; the wives were treated purely as vehicles for the sexual act:

He thinks women are created to please men. If he wanted me in bed, he'd just get on with it right away and then turn his back and go to sleep. If he doesn't want me he goes to sleep just the same, without a word. I feel like I've just lost my feelings. (*Iqbal*)

Listen, I've been married for twenty-two years. Since I got married, I've learnt about attitudes towards women. The minute a man finishes having sex with a woman he treats her differently. (*Fatin*)

I believe that companionship is more important. That is what I believe. Sex is just a five-minute thing. If husbands and wives understood each other, sex wouldn't affect the relationship much. It's true that I've read in magazines that sex is an important part of marriage and is sometimes the cause of divorce, but personally I don't agree with that. (*Salwa*)

Given these statements, it is no surprise that almost half the women said sex was an unpleasant duty for them.

It seems that the sex act is usually quick and women are probably left feeling frustrated, even though they do not recognize or admit it. Because the sex act is so brief, men are probably frustrated too. Layla (quoted at the end of Chapter 5) describes the result of sexual frustration among men in public. (This frustration is worsened by the fact that men have few opportunities for sex outside marriage other than prostitutes.) So although men find release in sex, it does not bring real fulfilment and satisfaction to either partner. This use of prostitutes also adds to the paradox of sex in Iraqi society. Most men have premarital sex only with prostitutes, who are regarded as cheap, filthy and dishonourable. In many cases the prostitute is forced to practise her trade for economic survival. But the man who seeks her services is regarded as 'a real masculine man who can indulge in sex as he pleases'; he continues to hold himself in high esteem.

This paradoxical belief has its origins in the family: although young children are discouraged from discussing sexual matters, adults tend to turn a blind eye when male teenagers show an interest in sex. Indeed, society expects the young male to seek out sexual encounters, and while his mother might inwardly disapprove, she has been conditioned to accept such interest as a necessary part of her son's socialization; it is believed that abstinence could seriously damage the boy. As in the West, men proudly discuss their sexual adventures. In Iraq, however, this is limited to women outside the family circle; to discuss relatives would not be honourable. Any woman so discussed is reduced to an object of disgust and is regarded publicly as deviant.

Women tend to put up with the situation–it would be beneath their dignity to beg for love and affection:

> He doesn't know much about how women should be treated. I don't think he deliberately mistreats me this way, but I don't know what to say. Sometimes I think he's maybe too busy, or something. Maybe you can beg for other things, but you can't beg for affection and love. (*Ibtihal*)

Sex is clearly a duty, based on limited knowledge, and prostitutes are frequently the only sexual models that males encounter. However, these are not the only reasons for not showing love to the wife. The family hierarchy stresses the importance of a lover never having sexual intercourse with his beloved. Marriage is religiously sanctioned sexuality, not the union of two lovers.

Sex and Love

Classical Arabic literature has many references to a romantic or platonic love known as Udrite love. Yet Udrite love is forbidden to women, and the Udrite lover never has sexual intercourse with his beloved. The famous poet Gamil was not allowed to marry his beloved Bouseaina who was betrothed to a hideous suitor in order to protect her. Qais was prevented from marrying Laila. Afra was eternally separated from her passionate lover, Orwa ibn Hizam.[8] Thus it is obvious that even non-sexual love is discouraged, the assumption being that the woman must have deliberately attracted her lover, and that such behaviour would bring dishonour on the tribe. In fact girls should not even allow their lovers to mention their names in poems, as this would bring them into disrepute. Udrite love is recognized as the only honest love.

But the Udrite lover cannot marry as marriage involves sex. Thus once again, marriage appears to be divorced from love.

Physical love, which involves sexual attraction or sexual feelings, might lead to a sexual act between two lovers. Thus it also tends to result in the separation of the lovers, because men do not trust girls who indulge in such behaviour. The belief is that if a girl 'does it with them' she will 'do it with others'. Any girl acting in this way would not be trusted to be a good wife. This partly explains the segregation of the sexes in Arab society. Furthermore, Arab sexual mores assume that whenever a man and a woman find themselves alone, they will be driven to have sex.[9]

Women in Arab culture are sexually oppressed and isolated, full freedom being given only to men; there is no balance in relationships between the sexes. As El Saadawi notes, true love is based on an exchange between equal partners, but men and women are not equal in Arab society. Women are oppressed by men; they are passive and self-sacrificing. The structure of society itself makes true love an impossibility.[10] Thus even in present-day Iraq, the connection between sex and love is not strong; indeed, in most cases there is no such connection. The expression 'love-making' or 'make love' has no equivalent in modern Arabic, nor does it exist in classical Arabic, or in the various regional languages throughout the Arab world.

It might seem from the answers the women gave me that there is no love at all between spouses. There may be love, but it is not expressed, certainly not in the ways it is expressed in the West. It is considered to be very private, even for husbands and wives; they are not encouraged to show love to each other in front of other people–it would be considered dishonourable on the part of the wife and a weakness if it came from the husband. Even when the couple are on their own, love is not expressed due to reasons connected with upbringing, lack of models, and so on. Husbands assume that for them to show affection might 'spoil' the wife, who would take advantage of them and become demanding. This was confirmed by Majida's words at the beginning of this chapter quoting her husband: 'Women who hear soft talk misbehave.'

However, women are now becoming more aware of Western customs, through television and films. They expect their husband to show affection in ways which are not customary for Arabs:

I've never felt any love or affection from him. We've been married for sixteen years. Even by mistake, he's never told me how he feels. Sometimes I get very depressed, but he never asks what's wrong, he never suggests we go out, or takes us for a picnic. Sometimes in the spring, when the sun's shining and it's a beautiful day, we all feel like going out. He's got a car which I'm not allowed to drive. He takes the car and goes out, but he never takes me or the children anywhere. (*Muna*)

He doesn't show any feelings towards me. My father died when I was very young and my mother had to bring all of us up on her own, so she was very tired and didn't have enough time for us. I wish she'd been able to spare more time and we could have grown closer. I thought a husband would give me the love I had missed, but unfortunately he doesn't. Luckily he's faithful and stays in at home with me more often than he goes out. I swallowed my pride and reminded him the week before the date of my birthday. He still forgot, although later he said he was sorry. Then a week afterwards he suggested we celebrate my birthday. I didn't say anything but I was very hurt. Whenever I blame him for this sort of behaviour he reminds me of people who are much worse off than us. Then I tell him about the things I would like. I make it clear that I'm not concerned with furniture or other valuables of that nature, but then how can I make him understand? (*Rafida*)

The reason for such diversity in emotional reactions between men and women may be found in patterns of child-rearing. Men are taught from childhood to be tough and not to express affection, which is seen as a sign of weakness. This does not apply to expressing anger, however, which is linked very strongly with the notion of masculinity.

When I asked the women whether their husbands were affectionate, the majority said that not only were they not affectionate, they hardly ever expressed feelings of love. However, a few of them said that their husbands had expressed some love and affection before marriage while they were engaged. A few women said their husbands expressed love to them, on certain occasions, mainly with gifts and sometimes with sweet words.

Not only do Iraqi husbands not show affection to their wives, they are actually aggressive towards them:

He's very irritable and short-tempered. If he's angry about something he never goes to sleep until he's shouted at us and made a scene, particularly at me and my daughter. He behaves a little better with the boys. When he gets angry, he really gets angry; I mean he loses all control. Sometimes he comes home like that and takes it out on us. I try my best to calm him down by doing everything he wants, his way, but even that doesn't work with him. He gets better, then he does it again. I really don't know what else I can do. I obey all his orders. If he says don't go to your parents even if I badly want to, I won't. What more can I do to satisfy him? (*Muna*)

Almost all the women indicated that their husbands were irritable or bad-tempered:

He expresses his anger by endless shouting. (*Suha*)

He's always irritable. I can't possibly talk to him, sober or drunk. It's regrettable that I can't talk to him as other people do. I prefer to confide in my friends and talk to them about my problems, rather than my husband. (*Khadija*)

He's quick to express anger. (*Lutfia*)

He's always irritable and short-tempered. (*Amina*)

It is in the nature of Arab culture for people to show their emotions. But emotions themselves are gender-specific. Women are expected to show anger by complaining and weeping, while men shout and act irritated with their wives. What they are in fact doing is proving their masculinity, and exercising their control over their wives.

Society operates a double standard as far as morals are concerned, recognizing only male sexuality. Moreover, this sexuality is regarded as sacred. The idea that women's sexuality and passionate nature, once aroused, will prove to be too strong to control, and could threaten the whole of the social system, is still a powerful force behind the treatment of women and the behaviour of men. This idea dies hard and is still very prevalent in Iraqi society. If a woman feels any sexual desire it must not be admitted, even to her husband. I only found two exceptional women who cautiously admitted to feelings of sexual desire:

Frankly, in our society, men play the positive role in sexual relations and women are supposed to play the passive or negative one. I disagree with this, but if I make a positive approach, he backs off. I don't know why. Maybe it's due to his relations with a prostitute before we got married. He doesn't like it coming from me, because he considers his wife should act the opposite of these women. Whenever he wants intercourse with me, I respond in order to please him, even if I don't feel like it. I believe it's my duty. If I don't satisfy him, I might lead him to have affairs with other women, or he might try to harm me by acting against my interests in other daily matters, so I respond to avoid problems. (*Rafida*)

He doesn't really care much about how I feel. I don't discuss this with him because, for me, it's a matter of keeping some dignity, even though I think it's very important, and I try to drop hints by talking nicely to him when we go to bed, but he acts like he just wants me to shut up. No response at all. I always try to wear my sexiest nightgowns and make-up and perfume, but it doesn't seem to make any difference to him. When he wants sex, he demands it, ignoring my feelings. I get very upset about it sometimes. It really makes me depressed, but then I get over it. As a matter of fact, I do believe that it's my right too, but I feel shy talking about it with him. . .

I'm very sensitive and if I hear any bad news I'm upset for many hours. My husband is different. He's not emotional and he doesn't show any sensitivity or courtesy to me. He's cold and doesn't show his emotions. If I talk to him about it, he says, 'We're no longer children or at the beginning of our relationship, to show any feelings.' Mind you, he didn't show me any feelings even when we were engaged. He doesn't show any emotion towards me, no love, not even a word, whereas I wanted someone I could communicate with, who would spoil me and love me. Sometimes I tell him I used to be spoiled at home and my father loved me a lot. Now I feel deprived of all that. He just says, 'I'm not your father. I can't help it if your life was like that. I'm not used to that kind of thing.' (*Ansam*)

4
Relationships

Companionship in Marriage

Nowadays women in Iraq are beginning to expect the kind of companionable marriage between equal partners which the media have depicted as being the norm in Western society. This is in contrast to tradition, according to which women are expected to be subordinate. In my interviews, however, I was more concerned with the wives' adjustment to marital life and their position as women than with the amount and quality of happiness they found in marriage.

The Western conception of marriage as companionship derives from the concept of adulthood in Western societies. The individual separates from his or her natal family at a relatively early age and then has comparatively weak ties with them and thus sees the spouse as a primary companion. Even more important, perhaps, marriage partners in the West choose each other, and thus the relationship is based on friendship from the outset. In Iraq, however, marriage partners are chosen differently. Family ties are still very strong and individuals, particularly women, remain much closer to their natal family than to their own developing nuclear one. Very rarely do men or women separate from their family just for the sake of being independent;

they both expect to remain at home until marriage. Therefore, companionship in marriage is not valued as highly, particularly if we consider the lack of equality between husbands and wives. In conducting research on Iraqi society in the 1960s, the American researcher Elizabeth Fernea observed that the women in the village pitied her. She had no children, no long hair, no gold, was far from her mother, 'thin as a rail' and couldn't cook rice. Though they pitied her, she was, in her own words:

> college educated, adequately dressed and fed, free to vote and to travel, happily married to a husband of my own choice who was also a friend and companion. The idea of a husband as a friend had never occurred to my friends in El Nahra [a southern Iraqi village].[1]

It had never occurred to the women whom Fernea interviewed to regard a husband as a friend. This seemed to be true for the women I spoke to as well (particularly the housewives and teachers), in spite of the time gap and other differences between the two groups interviewed.

In Iraq and most other Arab countries, it is not customary for a husband and wife to use terms of endearment; even simple words of appreciation such as 'please' and 'thank you' are not used. Nevertheless a wife might say, 'May God lengthen your life, do so and so for me' if she is desperate for her husband's help. The Arab assumes that the wish has already been granted. However, it is not customary for the husband to say the same thing to his wife, particularly in the presence of other people, as it is his wife's duty to serve him. This may partly explain the tension between husbands and wives, which affects the way they interact with each other in everyday life.

Since a companion is someone you talk to, I was particularly interested in the women's day-to-day conversations with their spouse. I asked them, 'Do you feel you can talk to your husband quite easily? Do you talk about things that worry you? What sort of things can you discuss with him?' The majority found it extremely difficult to find a common topic of conversation apart from household matters or the children. Some women felt that if they started any conversation at all with their husband, it might end in an argument and then a fight. Iqbal, for example, felt that her husband did not trust her; he was suspicious and accused her of needing sympathy and of feigning illness in order to gain attention:

It isn't easy to talk. He's always suspicious. If I told him I was ill and needed a doctor, he'd say, 'There's nothing wrong with you!' He challenges me as to whether or not he has looked after me. I don't try to tell him my problems, because I know he's short-tempered and he'll eventually blame me for the problems.

Several other women indicated that they deliberately avoided conversation with their husband as, in most instances, it led to a fight.

As discussed in greater detail in the previous chapter, many husbands displayed signs of irritability within their marriage. Some of the women felt that their husband's need to be authoritative was displayed in ways which merely increased the wives' anxiety. By 'ridiculing' and 'picking on' them, they alienated their wives, who then felt unable to converse freely with their husbands. Several women stressed this point:

No, he doesn't allow me to speak. He's always making fun of me and doesn't show any flexibility. I'd like to talk to him about my problems, but he interrupts me. He listens to the radio or something, and couldn't care less. I occasionally talk to friends about my problems, but only those I can trust. (*Amina*)

Muna went into more detail, relating her husband's attitude to the way she got married and regretting not being able to leave him after her engagement:

He married me for my father's money. We didn't know about this. Or rather, we discovered it during the engagement period but we thought breaking the engagement meant divorce, because we had had a full ceremony from the beginning.

He's a very selfish person. He comes home late, and takes his frustrations out on me and my children. He realized from the beginning that I was as obedient as my mother, and took advantage of me. I was submissive, young and beautiful. He was 37 years old, but they told us he was 28. After the marriage ceremony, when I found out, everybody said, 'So what? An older man will look after you, take good care of you,' but he was merely a complicated, childish person. He had a superiority complex and always dreamt of wealth. He's never satisfied, despite the fact that we don't need any money. He always refutes my ideas. I have to support his ideas, otherwise I get into trouble. Even our children are surprised when they see me supporting him. I have to prepare breakfast and a packed lunch for him and for the children every single morning. Despite all this hard work, he blames me for paying more attention to the children than I do to him.

However, these attitudes take different forms. Several of the women told me their husbands hardly listened to them at all when they tried to speak. Even those husbands who did listen seemed bored and wished their wife to finish talking as soon as possible:

He's always reserved, but I always want to say what occurs to me without reservations. He listens to me, but doesn't seem to take any notice of what I say. We see each other for about two hours a day, but he isn't the type who understands or takes any notice. (*Fatima*)

He doesn't take part in any conversation with me. He just listens. I think he'd like me to keep quiet. (*Salwa*)

I don't feel he cares about what I say. (*Samar*)

Similarly, two women who were housewives stated that they did not talk to their husbands because they did not wish to bother them:

Why should I bother him? He doesn't like to talk. He always says, 'Let me rest.' (*Nadira*)

Feryal raised the question of the concept of manhood and how this relates to men's communication with women, which to some extent is considered degrading:

Yes, I can talk to him, but I doubt if he pays any attention to what I say. I think that's because of our concept of manhood. We think that's how a man should be. My submission to him has encouraged him to get away with a lot of things.

Many of the women said that they always thought hard and chose the moment carefully before engaging in any kind of conversation with their husband; despite this, many pointed out that their husband hardly ever took their opinions seriously:

I think he feels that I couldn't suggest any logical solution to any problems he comes across . . . I do have conversations with him, but he doesn't always take my opinion seriously. His own views are the only ones that he goes by. I sometimes tell him about things that have happened at school. I don't always talk to him about my personal affairs. Anyway he doesn't seem to be interested. In general, he doesn't talk much, and if he has any spare time, he tends to spend it repairing things at home, which takes hours and gives him a lot of satisfaction. I try to make jokes to attract his attention, but he replies that I'm a big baby, so I tend to withdraw and be silent.

Q: Why don't you talk to him about your personal affairs?

A: It's better not to talk to a husband about such things. It may create more problems. (*Ansam*)

Many of the women raised similar points, suggesting that they did not have confidence in their husbands and were afraid to reveal personal problems, particularly any connected with the natal family, for fear that the husband might use such information against them:

> I don't talk to him about my private affairs. I show him my best side, not my passive one. If I criticize him or his family, I have to bear in mind that he might refer to my problems or my family's, so I don't tell him all my problems. (*Nazira*)

> No, I can't talk to him easily, as he doesn't understand things easily. My conversations with him might lead us into trivialities. I don't reveal anything personal, because he doesn't co-operate with me. Besides he gossips to other people about what I say. (*Fadwa*)

> I talk to him about quite a few matters but not my family affairs as he's a stranger to them. (*Gamila*)

Husbands as Outsiders

The lack of confidence displayed by some of the women is

strongly linked with the notion of the husband being an 'outsider'.[2] Since the Iraqi family generally considers the son-in-law as an outsider, they teach the daughter to be discreet about her family and not reveal any of their personal affairs or secrets to him, for fear he would use them against her later.[3] It should be noted that the tie between brother and sister is much stronger than the husband/wife bond. Also the mother/son bond is much stronger than the husband/wife bond, or perhaps more highly valued socially: such ties are for a lifetime, unlike those between husband and wife which could always end in divorce, seen as 'an easy thing to do' for a man. Nahida went into more detail about this issue:

I never reveal personal information to him; I'm afraid he might use it to hurt my feelings. Whenever we have a fight, he mentions my sister who is mentally ill and says, 'I'm not surprised at your behaviour, what about your sister?' My other sister died in an accidental fire. We had a fight shortly after that fire, and he said, 'I don't believe your sister had an accident.' He believed the fire was deliberately started by her husband who wanted to get rid of her because she was disobedient, big-headed and impolite. I really wish he knew nothing about my family. It hurts me a lot when he talks like this; that's why I hide information from him.

This sort of behaviour, like others discussed elsewhere in this book, is indicative of the manipulation and mental violence against wives which seems to affect them profoundly. One could hardly say that such husbands and wives are friendly companions. Moreover, many of the housewives' stories revealed instances of physical violence against them.

I also wanted to discover the other side of the coin—whether husbands discussed personal problems with their wives. When I asked, 'What about your husband, does he talk to you about his own personal problems, at work for example?', several women gave very similar answers:

> No, he says he doesn't want me to worry. I sometimes feel he's secretive and keeps things to himself. (*Hala*)

Some husbands generally did not talk a lot:

> In general he's calm and doesn't talk much. (*Salwa*)

Only one woman had a husband who confided in her about a very personal matter:

> He told me about his first wife. He divorced her because she couldn't have children. I didn't know this when I married him. Later on, he told me that she was immoral and obstinate and liked to go out a lot. This was why he divorced her and married me. (*Rahima*)

She did not seem to realize that perhaps he only revealed this information as a means of controlling her. The majority of women's husbands did not talk to them about their own personal matters.

Husbands who Drink

During the interviews, I became aware of an unexpected additional problem for the women: the high incidence of alcoholism among their husbands. This appeared to be the main reason why many wives objected to their husbands spending time outside the home. Although the official religion in most Arab countries is Islam and Islamic law forbids the consumption of alcohol in any form, many governments in Muslim countries are reluctant to ban it, perhaps for political reasons. There is a large market for a very strong, cheap drink called *arak*, which is mainly consumed by men. Men say they drink to release their problems; drinking is also seen as masculine behaviour. Moreover, it is taken as a sign that men have adopted modern attitudes, as opposed to traditional ones.

Most of the husbands spent long periods of their leisure time away from home, often engaging in heavy drinking bouts:

> I'd like him to stop drinking and stay in more with me at home. He's an alcoholic. He drinks every day. He comes home at 8 p.m. from work just to check whether everything is all right. Then he goes out again until 1 o'clock in the morning. If I talk to him about it he says, 'You can't stop me drinking.' I talked to my father. I told him, 'He's your friend, you know him well, why did you marry me off to him knowing he drinks?' He said, 'But he only used to drink once a week.' (*Majida*)

As in all societies, alcoholism creates many social problems, including violence within the family and the disruption of the home and family finances. While drinking is recognized as a social activity, it is one from which women are excluded. It is deemed dishonourable for a man to allow his wife to mix with his male drinking companions as they might act disrespectfully towards her, under the effect of alcohol. The consumption of alcohol, therefore, can be seen to create a gulf between a man and his family. Many Iraqi women also believe that the over-consumption of alcohol may lead to infidelity on the part of their husbands. Most of the women I interviewed said that their husbands or fathers (and in many cases both) were alcoholics.

Absent Husbands

The majority of women accepted their husbands going out with friends, as this was considered a normal thing for a man to do. The main feeling expressed when the husband went out alone or travelled on his own was one of relief:

> I don't miss him at all. (*Suha*)

> I'm often very happy when he's away. (*Fadwa*)

> I'm happy when he is travelling. (*Iqbal*)

> It would be much more peaceful without him. (*Khadija*)

Another typical answer came from Salwa, who wanted her husband to communicate with her, but knew this was not likely:

> I like being with him but not for too long at a time, as he doesn't talk much. I often meet my women friends and we go out together and talk on the telephone.

Fawzia's response was representative of most of the women:

> No, I don't feel at ease when he's at home. I try to keep myself busy to avoid any arguments.

Their husbands' absences affected them primarily in the areas of shopping and housekeeping, yet even this was taken care of:

> He buys everything before he leaves. (*Baidaa*)

> He provides everything for us. (*Sabiha*)

So far as these women were concerned, the husband's usefulness lay only in helping with the shopping or in carrying heavy things:

I do miss his help when he's away. When I carry the gas cylinder up the stairs to our flat, I find it extremely hard and I really wish he was around to help. (*Zahida*)

So the husbands are missed mainly for their physical help, and women find it more peaceful at home if they are not around–even though this contradicts their wish to keep them at home to prevent them from drinking.

Going Out Together

Due to the influence of modernization some educated women have begun to expect their husbands to stay at home; if going out they would go out together. Most of the clubs are for men only, however, and men still associate mainly in occupational clubs. Since the 1970s clubs for families have started to open. Urban middle-class couples in Iraq nowadays visit friends together, go to clubs and attend mixed parties, although this represents a break with tradition. Nevertheless, women find it very difficult to feel at ease in mixed company and so, probably, do the men.[4] At these parties or even when visiting friends, the men tend to gather together to discuss politics, business, and so on, while the women talk about fashion, cooking, their children and their everyday affairs, or perhaps gossip about other women. Most of the women I talked to found these topics silly and boring. However, they have to watch their behaviour and avoid talking or laughing loudly, sitting with their legs apart, and so on.

As mentioned above, women do not seem relaxed in such an atmosphere and do not gain much satisfaction from these experiences. This raises the question of the quality of such leisure activities, which hardly seems satisfactory to women. The reasons can be found both inside and outside the family. The family influences the husband's attitude, and he in turn restricts his wife with a multitude of rules relating to the way she talks, sits and dresses:

> I like going out with him but I don't like his attitude. He tells me not to laugh and how I should walk, etc. He's very jealous. (*Shada*)

Rafida's story illustrates another situation which is more serious but even more common:

> We go out together a lot; we sometimes visit friends or relatives. He hardly ever goes out alone. I'm very sociable and I used to love going out, but not any more. He pays attention to everybody else but me. He makes me feel so small when he shuts me up in front of people if I try to get involved in conversation. I long for the day when I can talk about anything, even something very small, and he will listen to me and treat me as he treats his friends.
>
> I don't have much faith in our relationship. Sometimes I tell him, 'To be honest, you're a successful man but you're a failure as a husband.' Of course, I shouldn't say it. He says, 'What have I deprived you of?' I never say anything but I wish, just once, that he'd bring me a small present or take me out for a meal, but he never does. He's influenced by his parents, who say that if a man gives a woman things she'll run away from him. He doesn't like me to go shopping on my own, but at the same time he doesn't like me to plan to go out as he has to give me a lift there and back: and that again, according to him, will make me spoiled. He's quite open about it. He's dominant, and it seems as if I'm encouraging him to be so, by not questioning his attitude to avoid problems. For example, I'd love to learn to drive. It's very important nowadays with the increasing transport problems in Baghdad, but he won't let me; he says he doesn't

want me to have an accident. I pretend that I agree with him, and leave it for a while and try again, but so far without success.

Several women thought their husband ridiculed them or ignored them in front of others. Coping with this kind of behaviour in a social situation, even if it does not occur all the time, is not conducive to a relaxed mood. Many women put on a 'respectable' act in the presence of other men, although it was not always clear what was considered respectable. In most cases, however, the men gathered on one side of the room and the women on the other, so they were segregated anyway. Men apparently find more comfort in the company of other men whom they regard as equals, while women are seen to enjoy the company of other women and to feel free to confide in them. According to one of the women attending the illiteracy eradication centre, one of the centre's greatest advantages was the chance to go out and meet other women. She would not have been able to do so if her husband were not obliged by law to allow her out.

In comparison, all-female activities and outings are much more relaxed, although most women see themselves and their husbands as 'liberated' only if they go out in mixed groups. Here again, modernization has brought a conflict for women. Leisure should bring happiness and satisfaction, and be something to look forward to. The changes which transfer women from the segregated world in which they used to live to the mixed atmosphere of modernity do not, according to the majority of these women, improve the quality of their lives. The important question is not whether they have the possibility of outside socializing, but whether it brings them a feeling of relaxation and enjoyment. Many of the women I spoke to who felt these experiences were unsatisfying saw this at an individual level, blaming their luck and their marriage.

Women and Leisure

Not all the women were in agreement as to what constituted a leisure activity. For instance, housework qualified as leisure for some women, while for Maisoon and Rafida attending parties was not their idea of relaxation. Leisure time is an important part of Iraqi men's life which hardly exists for women. For them, it consists mostly of going to visit friends and being free to visit their parental families, to which they are very close. Indeed, this is the main activity open for them, since most outdoor activities are for men only, or for women only when accompanied by men.

Most of the activities Western women take for granted are not available to their counterparts in Iraq. Sport and swimming are not yet socially accepted for women and there are no evening classes in crafts or academic subjects–all learning has to be through schools and colleges with a certificate at the end.

The picture that emerged from my interviews ties in with other research on Iraqi women.[5] Most women with jobs find it extremely hard to go out and socialize with friends due to the double burden of work and housework. Sometimes they find it difficult to see even their own families and relatives. This is a particularly important issue. Even the most liberated men seem to prefer their wives to stay at home, simply in order to do more housework and to look after the children. A few women even said that when their husbands go out they say that they are leaving their wives to 'enjoy themselves working freely round the house'.

A husband may also want to prevent his wife meeting other people who might broaden her experience of life, which might then be used against him; this is particularly true of knowledge gained from her own parental family. As discussed earlier, husbands are considered to be outsiders. Since family ties are strong and wives do not confide in their husbands, they have to turn to their own families when problems arise. This alone is a threat to the husband, who may prevent his wife from visiting her parents.

Other leisure activities that are common in the West are virtually unknown to Iraqi women, particularly occupations at home such as reading, painting, and so on. One might expect the husband to view these as more acceptable than outside activities, but the women do not see home pursuits as leisure. Their responses to my question, 'Do you feel you have enough leisure time?' generally revealed negative experiences:

No, and I never went out in the first place. I'm busy with my children but I'd like to travel and enjoy myself. I can't convince my husband of my wishes. (*Feryal*)

No, I never enjoy my life. I'd love to go out, but my husband doesn't take us. I don't know where to go with my three children. (*Suha*)

He doesn't allow me to go anywhere. If it wasn't for the school, I wouldn't even see the street. (*Majida*)

No, of course not, because he's never taken us out in his life. (*Rahima*)

Men are much freer and have more access to outside activities than women; they are interested in other men's conversation and ideas. As noted in a different context, men 'attend to and treat as significant only what men say'.[6] This helps to explain the behaviour of Iraqi husbands. By communicating with other men outside, they gain a kind of satisfaction which is not available in the home. This partly explains why they spend most of their leisure hours away from home.

Research on Turkish women reveals a similar picture to that in Iraq:

> The interview reminded me of lonely, lower-middle-class Istanbul housewives who complain that their husbands never take them to the theatre or restaurants or parties but spend all their leisure time with their men friends at the coffee shop. Aside from visits to mother, these women say, they have little social life of their own . . . Each is trapped inside her own apartment . . . The best of the harem tradition–the companionship and support of other women–has disappeared . . . The problem lies mainly in the fact that after centuries of harem tradition, which kept sexes apart during most of the day . . . men and women have to relate intensely with each other for the first time in history. Young couples in small urban apartments find that they have to be more than sexual partners and draw almost all of their daily emotional nourishment from each other. This is utterly new to them. There are no local models to follow.[7]

One could argue that if a woman's husband is not strict, and has no objections to her going out, why does she not just take the children and go? This may be possible for Western women, but for an Iraqi woman the situation is completely different. She is brought up to feel insecure without a man and to be absolutely dependent, to the extent that some women feel proud of saying that they are frightened to go out alone. Coupled with the lack of transport, this makes it unlikely that they would wish to go out at all. Although the great majority of women accept the idea of staying at home and giving up leisure, it is worth asking whether they do so willingly:

> I enjoy my life generally. I have no leisure time, and my

concentration is always on the home and my children. It is true that he doesn't normally allow me to go out, but if I insist on going, I reassure him about the people I'm going to visit. He would then agree on allowing me to visit these people. But how can I leave my children and leave home when he's not there? (*Sabiha*)

I don't have time for leisure; I have lots of responsibilities at home. (*Amina*)

Since women appear to have almost no leisure time, and certainly not with their husbands, the question arises as to whether they want to spend time together at all. Most of the women I interviewed thought their husbands were irritable and fussy, and frequently 'picked on them'. At the same time, they wanted them to be at home more, so that they could prevent them drinking. I asked, 'Do you like spending your spare time with your husband? If so, how?' Most of the answers confirmed that the husband spent most of his time away from home, despite the wife's wishes to the contrary:

I wish he'd stay at home or that we went out together but he doesn't agree. (*Suha*)

I would have been happy to stay in at home with him but instead I hardly see him. (*Labiba*)

I wish we could either stay at home together or go out together but he goes out on his own every day and gets drunk. I started suspecting him and asked some people to keep an eye on him. They told me that he goes out with other men for a drink after work. (*Majida*)

Looking at these answers in isolation from the women's experiences in other aspects of life, one might think they wanted the husband to stay at home because they enjoyed his company. Majida's explanation–that she did not want her husband to drink– is perhaps closer to reality. When husbands often go out drinking, it causes their wives anxiety, while they tend to be 'stuck at home' with the children.

It is important at this point to discuss the problem of transport, particularly for working women who appear to be less restricted by their husbands. Most of the working women I spoke to needed to be able to drive and complained that their husbands refused to allow them to learn. Some of them saw this disapproval as their husbands' fear that they might gain some independence. (Despite this control, most women found ways of seeing their natal family frequently.) The husbands gave various reasons and excuses for preventing their wives from learning to drive:

> I'd like to learn how to drive a car but I can't because he objects. His excuse for not letting me drive is that our roads are uneven, there are a lot of road works and they're crowded, so he worries about me having an accident, but I'm not convinced by all this. I've often tried to make him change his mind, but no way. (*Sabiha*)

> When he bought a car, he kept on saying that I was not suited to driving because I have a bad temper. He kept on saying this for ten years. When we moved to another area and I *had* to learn to drive, I was very frightened and hesitant. (*Hala*)

Fatima was in a similar situation. She also wished that her husband would pay more attention to her feelings (which is again a Western kind of behaviour):

114

He doesn't let me learn to drive. I'd find it very useful. If I want to buy something he doesn't agree and says it's not important. If his parents or anyone else said it was worth buying, he would. This makes me hate him. With me, he's very mean. He forgets to buy me a present on my birthday and says he has provided me with a house and furniture–this is my present. He's never bought me a personal present in my entire life with him. He says I have my own salary! He tries to get his hands on my salary but I don't let him. I try to make him feel guilty by buying presents for him. My mother gave me a birthday party and he said I was spoilt, that these things are rubbish. He criticizes what I wear or what make-up I put on. When I sit I shouldn't cross my legs and when I enter a room I shouldn't say 'hello', but 'good evening'. I feel time is going so slowly. Four months with him seem like twenty years. He says, 'I want children but if they cry take them to the other room.' I can't bear it!

It might be argued that having a car, or having fewer children, would give a woman more opportunities for leisure. But if the husband does not allow her out to visit friends, a car would make no difference. And at least the children provide her with an excuse for visiting her own natal family.

Relationship with the In-Laws
Marital relationships in Iraq are further complicated by the fact that brides traditionally made their home with their husband's natal family–this was still the case for some of the women I interviewed. The husband's commitment to his natal family, whether financial or otherwise, and his family's involvement in his and his wife's private affairs, can create problems. With the coming of the nuclear family, however, many of the women were experiencing the 'in-law problem', that is, the wife's continuing loyalty to her own natal family, over and above what the husband

thinks is reasonable, and the perceived interference of the wife's relatives in the couple's private affairs. Once again, Westernization has brought new problems without necessarily solving the old ones. The nuclear family has been one of the most important results of women's participation in the workforce, as women's wages mean that they and their husbands can afford to live separately from their in-laws. This is a source of pride for the couple. When a man asks for a girl's hand and promises to provide a separate house for her, that is considered a privilege. Iraqi women believe that no educated woman would agree to live under her in-laws' control.

In Chapter 1, the strong ties within families were discussed. These ties are stronger between women and their parental families than between men and their own natal families. Women are aware of the tension between their husbands and their own relatives, and this again leads to tension between the spouses themselves, as revealed in the quotations below. Women may seem closer to their own parents than do their husbands because of the socialization process. Women are brought up to be dependent on the family, which exercises full social control over them. If a woman is close to her family, she will always turn to them for advice; this gives them the authority to control her, as well as keeping her dependent. Problems between husband and wife usually result in the wife turning to her family. Thus she sees them as something to fall back on when she has problems, although they control her at the same time. Men's upbringing is different as there is no need to control them. This explains the husband's suspicion of his wife's family: he cannot always punish his wife and get away with it. If he wished to 'teach her a lesson', her family might act as a restraining influence:

Although he's my husband, he's an outsider to me, and not my flesh and blood. I was very ill once, I visited a large number of

clinics. Some doctors advised me to have an operation. My
health was getting worse. My husband was accusing the
doctors of robbing me. I was on the verge of death and didn't
know what to do until my sister visited me. (My mother had
died and I only have this one sister.) My husband was drafted to
the army at that time and only heard about me a week later. My
sister took me to hospital and I was operated on straight away.
She had to borrow some money to pay for my medical
expenses, as she had no money herself. I was extremely ill. I
was cured by a miracle, and my husband didn't know anything
about what was going on, as he was away, thank God.
Otherwise he would've stopped me from having the operation.
I had to keep my children with me at the hospital, as there was
nowhere else for them to go. When he visited me, he was cool;
he didn't thank my sister. He told me I'd been a fool to spend
my money on unnecessary operations. He accused me of being
stupid, having my stomach opened up for the sake of the
operation. I just looked at him, unable to say a thing. When he
left I started weeping. (*Zahida*)

His relationship with my family is very bad. He hates them.
Once, years ago, my sister was very critical of him and even
now he still remembers it. He's a malicious person. My mother
always tells me to look after him and his family. I used to live
with his family and was very kind to them. I wanted to prove
that the myth about the daughter-in-law was nonsense so I
tried to be part of them, but in return he hated my family's guts.
However, once when I needed his family's help they didn't
respond. Another time I had a bad quarrel with him–I left and
went to my parents' house, but he didn't come to me to be
reconciled. He was awarded a scholarship to study in Egypt, so
he left without consulting me. When the school term started, I
had to return to his parents' home as my work was in the same

city as them and my parents lived in another city. This is life, what can I do? (*Feryal*)

Despite the fact that almost half of the women interviewed lived with their in-laws at the start of their marriage, not all had found it difficult to adjust. The main reason for living with in-laws is financial–the nuclear family is nowadays considered preferable. I asked the women: 'How do your parents get on with your husband?' 'What about his parents?–do you get on well with them?'

I try to be nice to his mother although she treats me badly. He hates my family. He doesn't respect them and won't even eat in their house when he's invited. (*Suher*)

Although they're my uncle and aunt, and they always say I'm different from their other daughters-in-law as they're not relatives, my parents-in-law don't treat me well. When I go to work I leave my baby with them. When I come back they force me to do lots of housework in return, even though there are so many women living there and they could always give me less to do if they divided the work equally between us. They never allow me to leave the baby with them for even a few minutes after work. (*Shada*)

His family used to treat me very badly until I had my first baby; they must have thought I couldn't have children. They're all right now that I've had another one and they're both boys. (*Rahima*)

His sister always makes trouble for me. She tries to control everything in the house. Now my son is married and she makes trouble between me and my daughter-in-law. I try to stay quiet and remember that she was young when her husband divorced her and threw her out; she had nowhere else to go. Although she's a difficult person, I have to be patient. I pity her. Just imagine, he gets jealous when he sees that I have a good relationship with his family, because he has a bad relationship with both his own and my family. But what can I do? I've lived with my sister-in-law ever since I got married and now I'm used to it. (*Fawzia*)

Suher was living with her husband's mother while Fawzia was with her husband's sister. In both cases, the female in-law had nowhere else to go, as a single woman is not allowed to live alone in Iraqi society. As for the other women quoted above, they lived with their in-laws because they had only married recently and could not yet afford to be independent.

The women I met seemed to believe that there is more tension between a man and the powerful figures in her parental family than between a woman and her husband's family. The following quotation indicates that the traditional conflict between a wife and her in-laws does not exist in most modern nuclear Iraqi families:

My family doesn't hurt him despite what he's done to me. When they criticize him he's embarrassed. When I get cross and stay with my family for a few days, they try to reconcile us, but he says, 'How can I face them? I feel embarrassed.' His family are very kind and treat me nicely and they try to be on my side. Sometimes when I'm cross, I go to his family to relax. I like them too. (*Jamila*)

The close relationship between the wife and her natal family leads to tension not only between the husband and the wife's family but also between husband and wife:

I don't live with my in-laws. I visit them now and then. They feel sorry for me. When my sisters visit me and see his behaviour they cut the visit short and leave. (*Khadija*)

The majority of the women lived near their own natal family. As it is against Iraqi traditions for a man to live with his wife's family, only one woman lived with her parents at the beginning of her marriage, and this was exceptional. In this case the husband and wife were cousins and both worked in Baghdad where her family lived. As his family did not live in Baghdad, the couple needed to build their own house. While doing so they lived with her family.

Iraqi men are nevertheless expected, with some limitations, to form a relationship with their wife's family. A husband is expected not to avoid his in-laws, but rather to live with his family near them or his own family if possible, while a wife prefers to live near her own family.

Several women told me that their husband also had a poor relationship with his own family, in several cases even before marriage:

He used to treat his mother in a way which clearly meant that he didn't care much for her. I stopped visiting his family because of his bad behaviour with both his family and my own. I personally like his family and I have particularly strong ties with my family. (*Fadwa*)

His relationship with his family is quite cold. (*Sabiha*)

He doesn't have any respect for women. His mother used to tell me about his cruelty to his sisters; he used to beat them. Once, his brothers got really fed up with him and threw him out of the house. He even used to hit his mother. Would you believe it if I told you that we've been living in this house for twelve years and his family live in the next street? He hasn't been to visit them once in all these years. (*Sahira*)

If his family visits us, he always argues or fights with them and makes them leave the house. (*Khadija*)

He loves his mother but he doesn't take any notice of what she says. He doesn't show any respect for his sisters. (*Suha*)

Since the family has traditionally been an extended one in Iraq, a cousin would also be a member of the family. Jamila wished she had married a cousin as this would have offered some sort of protection—a cousin would not swear at her as it would refer to his own family. She put it like this:

My husband ignores me, hitting me and humiliating me. He's always very irritable. He's very clumsy. He doesn't care about cleaning or tidying up at all, unlike me, so if I clear up and he comes looking for a paper or something and can't find it he makes life hell, swearing at me. He's jealous. He doesn't like anyone talking to me, even his own mother, fearing that I might learn things. I sometimes regret my marriage and wish I'd married a relative who at least knows me. Then, if he swore at me it would be against his own family. If he'd been a cousin of mine, we wouldn't have lacked anything. I married a stranger who swears at me and my family, insults me and is ill-mannered at home. I'm extremely sorry and regret my marriage. (*Jamila*)

There is another reason for such conflict. Many women give money to their natal family, and this can be a source of great discontent to the husband, leading to conflict between the partners. Because working wives need the support of their own family, it is important that they keep in close contact with them. Women who do not work outside the home also need their family's support, in one way or another. When I asked the women, 'What sort of things do you think about which worry you the most?', an even clearer picture emerged of the strong bond between a woman and her natal family:

> Problems at work upset me sometimes, I mean it makes me think a lot about them, but mainly I worry about my brothers. If one of them has a problem, it would be as if it were my problem more than his. (*Salwa*)

> I'm so emotional. I always think about my mother and the family. I get worried about them. I either see them or telephone them every single day. (*Suhad*)

> What I think about mainly is my children's work at school, and how to improve it. I also think a lot about my [natal] family. (*Samar*)

> I feel as though I'm responsible for my brothers and sisters, and even their children, as if they were all mine. They take up most of my thoughts. (*Fadwa*)

Consequently tension is created between the couple, because the wife's close ties with her natal family and the support she receives from them in turn reduce the husband's exclusive control over her. Thus in Iraq the traditional conflict between a wife and her in-laws is replaced by a conflict between the husband and his in-laws.

Important Events in a Woman's Life

This attachment to the natal family was also revealed through another question: 'What, in your opinion, is the most important thing that's happened in your life, and why?' When I asked this question, I expected a wide range of answers. However, the majority of women mentioned the death of one of their parents:

> The most important event in my life was the death of my father, which affected and upset me very deeply. (*Samar*)

> My father's death, though he was living far away, but he used to support me when I needed him. (*Fawzia*)

The death of other family members was also mentioned. This confirms the deep-rooted ties with the parental family, making the loss of a close relative a deeply felt pain in a woman's life.

Many women were not clear as to what the question meant. I explained, 'an important thing that has changed your life'. Some of them asked, 'A change for the better or the worse?' I replied, 'Either'. To my surprise, very few women mentioned marriage. I had expected them to see their marriage as the major event, since most of them clearly felt that it had changed their life not only dramatically, but also for the worse.

Only one woman made the distinction between a positive and a negative event:

> The most important negative thing that has happened to me was the death of my mother, and the most important positive one was my marriage and the birth of my child. (*Sumia*)

And Muna said:

> Maybe one of the most important things was building our

house. I was happy then. As a matter of fact, I was very happy about that, but my happiness didn't last long, as we paid three-quarters of what it cost (I mean, me and my family). They helped to get us on our feet. I was hoping he'd put it in both our names, I mean half for me and half for him, but he insisted on claiming it for himself. This was a disaster in my life which upset me for a long time, as I don't really feel secure now, but I must consider the marriage as more important than that, because the bad relationship I have with him is the reason behind my wish to own a house.

Some (but by no means all) women regarded the birth of their children as the major event. Rahima saw 'getting pregnant' as the most important moment of her life. For Labiba, it was 'When God greened our home,' in other words, when she started having children. Most of the women who regarded childbirth as the major event in their life were illiterate housewives. However, many working women have very similar views. Nazira's answer below, and the even stronger views of other working women in Chapter 1, indicate that the birth of a male child is an important event for everyone:

> Giving birth to my children in the first place, and my marriage in the second place. The most important event in my life was when my sister-in-law gave birth to a baby boy after having difficulties for seven years. (*Nazira*)

Majida also indicated the importance of a male child and how worries about having a girl adversely affected her pregnancy. This was the worst and most enduring memory of her life:

> I was affected by my pregnancy. My sister wished I could have a boy. My husband threatened me and said he'd send me to my

parents if I gave birth to a baby girl, and that she'd be got rid of by throwing her down the drain. I was young, frightened and anxious at that time and only found out later that my husband was just teasing me.

Only two women mentioned their marriage as the most important positive thing in their life. Several others saw it as the major negative event:

My marriage is the most important thing that has happened to me. In a sense, it has affected my life very badly. (*Muna*)

Although graduation and starting work were also mentioned, the death of a member of the parental family was overwhelmingly the most important life event. Perhaps this is because it indicates loss of power for a woman, as every member of her parental family is a symbol of her strength. It may also be due to the social emphasis placed upon the family and how they should regard the loss of one of their members.

Death and the Mourning Period

Mourning is a very important social custom in Iraq, particularly in the central and southern areas; women play a major role. Iraqi society values the women who practise traditional mourning: dressed in black, they cry and beat their chests and heads, in other words, exaggerating their sadness on the death of a family member. The *aza* is a gathering of women to cry for the dead, usually lasting forty days, when the women of the house dress in black and, in some regions, wear the veil as a sign of mourning (whether or not they are traditionally veiled).

Older female relatives, such as grandmothers and aunts, stay in the house for forty days and can expect visitors at any moment. During these forty days, television, radio and all other sources of entertainment are forbidden. Visitors usually share in the sadness with them, crying and beating their chests,[8] for the first seven days of such sessions. Most of the women I spoke to had been involved in this traditional mourning practice; and for the first few days of the mourning period, they found the custom helpful as it provided an outlet for their grief and perhaps a way of releasing all their other problems as well. Towards the end of the forty days, however, it started to become a burden, especially the embargo on television. A woman would be frightened to turn the set on in case someone came in and discovered her.

As already mentioned, Arabs are generally emotional people. The expression of emotions, however, differs greatly from men to women, as revealed on the occasion of a death. Apart from escorting the body to the burial ground, the men of the house only hold three open days for visitors, while women hold forty. Men continue to sit on chairs and are comfortable, while women sit on long thin mattresses on the floor. Men drink coffee and listen to the Quran, either on tape or from someone hired to read it aloud. Meanwhile, women hire a *mulaya* or *naiha*, a woman who reads very little from the Quran but mainly sings laments, quotes certain sayings and calls upon the name of the deceased, in order to encourage people to cry. Women are expected to wear black for at least one year while men only wear a black tie for a few days. Outings like parties and visits to the cinema are forbidden to women for at least a year, the only exceptions being necessary trips, such as shopping and work. But men feel free to do as they please once the three days are over.

There is one positive aspect of the mourning tradition, apart from it providing an outlet for the woman's grief. It gives older women a more important role in the family, as shown by their leading part in the mourning ritual. For example, one of the women told me:

When my mother died her sister, who's the oldest woman in my mother's family, moved in with us from Basra for the forty days' mourning period. At the time I was very depressed, and on anti-depressants; every once in a while I'd start crying. Sometimes I cried at the wrong time according to my auntie. She used to tell me off after the people left, as I was supposed to cry with them at a certain time. One day one of the visitors stayed for a very long time waiting for her lift, so we served lunch while she was there, and my auntie was very cross because that happened on a day when we weren't supposed to eat in front of people. (*Fadwa*)

Women as well as men are socialized to be emotional, though in different ways. Men exaggerate their emotions (sometimes, as we have seen, by shouting at their wives and children), but this is not perceived as a sign of weakness. With women, however, although society encourages them to be emotional, this can sometimes work against them, since they are identified with traditional, backward practices such as crying for death. It can also be a disadvantage in their careers. One of the strongest reasons given for excluding women from positions of decision-making is that they are over-emotional. While the whole process of socialization encourages women to be emotional, they are penalized for their response. It is little wonder that women are often confused in a changing society.

5
Majida, Muna and Sabiha: Three Case Studies

Majida, Muna and Sabiha are three of the women I interviewed at length. It seemed interesting to give a picture of their daily routine in their own words. This provides some indication of the burden that falls on the Iraqi housewife (the issue of housework will be dealt with in more detail in Chapter 6).

Majida

When I first talked to Majida–a housewife aged 37–I noticed that her expression was rather sad and pained; she never smiled. (Later on I learned that she suffered from asthma.) She was, however, quite friendly and outspoken. The interview took place at the school she attended.

Majida was one of four sisters and two brothers (her brothers were at that time involved in the Iraq-Iran war). As children, her family had bought them clothes and food without being asked. However, they lived at their grandfather's house with their uncles, who treated her and her sisters very harshly. One of her uncles was a teacher, but despite this he only allowed her to attend school for three years. Her mother used to accompany her to and from school to prevent her uncles stopping and beating her. Her father spent much of his time abroad on business, so the uncles were able to exert more control over the family left behind. By the time Majida and her brothers and sisters reached adulthood, life with the uncles had become intolerable and their father moved them into a rented house. The two younger sisters then started school while Majida had to become a wife and mother.

She got married at the age of 16 but when I spoke to her she did not look much older than her own children. Majida had three daughters and three sons. The eldest, a girl, was in her final year studying science at the University of Baghdad, while the youngest was a boy of 6. The oldest son was in his last year of high school. Majida argued constantly with this son, who was rather rude and rough with her, unlike her youngest son who was more considerate. Her husband refused to interfere in such rows, and sometimes shouted at her, 'What do you want me to do? Shall I kill him?' They all lived in a five-bedroom house with a big garden in Baghdad owned by the husband.

Her husband was alcoholic and drank during office hours. She often thought about reporting him. She blamed her father for marrying her off to him, because he was her father's friend and he knew him very well. Her husband prevented her from going out or attending school, using their children as an excuse. When the Illiteracy Eradication Law was passed, her husband was forced to let her join such a school. She wanted to prove herself but was unable to complete her education, although she enjoyed going very much. Majida lived in fear of her husband who would threaten her with divorce if she showed the slightest sign of boredom, illness or being late from school. When she told her father this, he would say, 'He's all right, so long as he doesn't beat you.' And as long as her husband provided her with the essentials, her father advised her to keep herself busy with her children and leave her husband to his outside world. When she complained to her father about feeling bored and said she 'couldn't stand' her husband any longer as he did not allow her to go out, her father advised her to busy herself at home; since she had a big garden, she could always plant flowers or find something to do which would keep her busy and happy.

Her husband was very secretive. He never told her anything about his business, so she learnt about his work from other people. He would be co-operative when they invited friends to dinner, and she enjoyed those gatherings, as she felt he was closer to her than at other times. Majida regretted her marriage, but had chosen blind obedience and silence in preference to divorce.

When I asked her what she considered the most important event in her life, she sighed deeply and said she would never forget something her husband had said which affected her sleep for seven months. During the first months of her pregnancy her husband threatened to send her to her parents if she gave birth to a baby girl, and that he would throw the baby down the drain. Majida shed a lot of tears when she heard this, and lived in fear and anxiety until the birth. She gave birth to a girl, which was met with silence on the part of her husband. In subsequent years, she gave birth to boys, which met with his approval. On these occasions he celebrated by giving money to the poor and slaughtering a sheep.[1]

As for her daughter, Majida's husband did eventually become fond of her, although her brother still maintained that bringing up girls was very difficult; they were merely a burden on their family. Majida was resigned to these male attitudes and told me simply, 'All men are alike.' She gave me a detailed account of her daily routine:

I wake up at 6 in the morning. I start breakfast, then wake the children up, one after the other. While they dress, I take my husband a drink–a special kind of herb tea–in bed, then he starts getting ready. Meanwhile the children leave the house. He comes down and I have breakfast with him. After he leaves I start cleaning and washing up, then I start the daily housework. I clean the family room twice a day, also the toilet and the hall. The kitchen needs continuous cleaning. I clean the visitors' room once a week, unless we have visitors; then I have to clean it after they leave. At 11 o'clock, I start preparing lunch. The children arrive at different times so we don't all have lunch together, but I have to keep it warm from 1 until half past 2 when the last child eats. My husband has a nap after lunch. The children don't always take a nap, but I leave for school right after washing the dishes. It's a sort of relaxing time for me at school; I look forward to it. When school finishes, I go to my husband's work, which is nearby. I have to wait for a bit while he locks up and we go home together. He just comes home to check whether everything's all right, then he leaves with his friends. He doesn't have supper with us. He goes out drinking every evening, and then he comes home late for supper; sometimes he eats out. I start supper for the children and by 8 o'clock I've finished washing the dishes and cleaning, so I sit in front of the TV to do some sewing, altering clothes, knitting or sometimes ironing.

Muna

When I knocked on Muna's door, I found she was expecting me the following day. She apologized and asked me to excuse the house not being very tidy. I sat on the nearest chair in a room in which furniture was scattered about and children were playing. Then she invited me into the visitors' room, which was relatively tidy. She asked her 15-year-old daughter to bring me tea and cake while she went to her bedroom to change her dress and brush her hair.

Muna told me she had four children, one daughter and three sons. She was 36 years old and worked as a teacher. She seemed a very serious person. She was born in Baghdad to a conservative family who never allowed her to visit her friends. Her father was short-tempered and, while never physically punishing his children, constantly sought to impose his views on them and guide them towards what he thought was right. He did not allow the brothers to interfere in their sisters' affairs. Muna was the youngest of five sisters; her mother suffered mental anguish every time she gave birth to a girl, although she had six sons.

Muna had continued her high school education, but did not get good enough grades to attend university. Instead she enrolled at a teacher training college and graduated as a teacher. By law teachers have to start their career in schools outside the big cities,[2] except for married women, who stay with their husbands. Muna's two unmarried sisters had this problem after their graduation—each time their mother was forced to accompany them to their new homes, which were very far from Baghdad, thus abandoning her husband and the rest of the family. As a result, when Muna's turn came and she was appointed to a job 300 km away from home, her family accepted the first suitor who asked for her hand in marriage.

It was a traditional proposal: a high school teacher who was much older than her asked her to marry him. Muna saw herself as obedient, rich and beautiful, in addition to her good reputation and good upbringing. Her husband, however, was mainly attracted by her salary and her family's wealth. She did not realize this at first, so she was co-operative and her family contributed towards the furnishing of their home. Her husband had only 50 Iraqi dinars (approx. £100) when they got married, but she chose not to comment, thinking that her marriage would at last enable her to find a job in Baghdad.

During our conversation she described her husband as complicated, self-centred and short-tempered. He would not listen to other people or admit his own faults; he never helped with the housework or with the children. He drank and had smoked from an early age. Muna later learnt that his family had encouraged him to get married because they wanted to get rid of him. Soon after their marriage she began to realize what he was really like.

Whenever she complained to her mother about her unhappy marriage, her mother replied that all men were alike and she had to be tolerant. As a result Muna had grown to hate all men and had decided not to marry her own daughter off, thanking God that only one of her four children was a girl. Nevertheless, the influence of her own upbringing had its effect on the way she treated her daughter; she would not allow her to visit friends and warned her that being the only daughter, and having no sisters to discuss matters with, she would have to face the world alone if she did not stick to her mother and listen to everything she said.

Muna was exhausted by the double responsibility of being a teacher and a housewife. She felt her husband suffered from a superiority complex: he looked down on women and always refuted her opinions even when they were right and logical, forcing his own ideas on her. His conservatism and reactionary personality led him to mistreat his daughter. He once saw her talking outside their home to the neighbours' daughter while her brother was standing nearby. He rushed out and dragged her away by her hair, beat her severely and then drew a knife. Fortunately Muna was around to prevent him injuring her.

At the beginning of their married life, the husband used to lock Muna in the house. She had never forgotten being unable even to visit her neighbours because of her imprisonment. Muna soon lost her self-confidence, particularly with the neighbours, and he then abandoned the idea of locking the door.

He had no interest in his wife except in bed, although he became suspicious if a strange man stared at her. Every summer, without fail, he left his family behind and went off to enjoy his holidays alone. Muna could recall only one family holiday in eighteen years of marriage: it was not a success and the children preferred not to be with him. Even so, Muna felt that her husband was able to discipline the children where she could not, and therefore wanted him to be at home.

He never consulted her about anything. If she wanted to replace something at home he would disagree, even if it was to be paid for by her family. He even had their house built in his name, despite it being largely paid for by her family. Although she offered him everything she had, he refused to help her, not even by emptying his own ashtrays.

His relationship with his own family was not close. Muna had noticed this when comparing her husband's behaviour with the care and attention she lavished on her own children and her love for her own family of origin. She found it impossible to talk to her husband about her thoughts and feelings and frequently regretted their marriage, but did not want to separate from him because of the shame attached to divorce and for the sake of their children. Even so, she sometimes thought it would be the only solution and that their children would be better off with one happy parent than living with parents who were always having disagreements. When Muna became depressed her husband took her to a doctor, who told her that looking after the family was the cause of her problem. In fact, she thought that her husband was the reason for her depression.

In spite of her experience, Muna still maintained that men were more cultured, were better managers and had greater imagination than women. For her an emancipated woman was simply one who was lucky enough to be able to make joint decisions with her husband.

In discussing her daily routine Muna described in detail her husband's attitude towards the housework:

I usually wake up at 5 in the morning, prepare breakfast and make sandwiches for everybody, even him, despite the fact that I'm very busy in the morning. I even have to give him his cup of tea. If a child needs something while I'm busy with one of the others, he doesn't bother to help. As a matter of fact he'd blame me for paying more attention to the children than I do to him. Then we all go out.

I come home in the afternoon to start cooking and doing the housework. First, I cook lunch. We eat at 2 and have a nap, particularly if it's hot. This isn't regular for the children, but my husband can't do without it. I hardly have half an hour's rest. There are so many things to do in the house, and if any of the children aren't asleep, I can't rest worrying about them, so I have to be with them. Also if the children need anything at all, from help with their homework to clothes or food and so on, they always come to me. They don't ever think of going to their father. In the afternoon, I wash the dishes from lunch, then I start the housework. I clean, wash, dust and sweep the floor every single day. Then I start supper. Meanwhile my husband has his cup of tea and leaves. He goes out every single day and comes back quite late.

Sometimes my mother or sisters come over; they help me when they come. I don't go to them as often, not only because he doesn't approve, but also because of the children. It's not easy to go out with them and it's impossible to go without them. In the evening I hardly manage to sit and watch TV or rest. By 9 o'clock I feel exhausted and I just want to go to bed.

Sabiha
Sabiha was a 28-year-old teacher with two sons and two daughters, all living in a small rented two-bedroom house. She was sociable and very pleasant to talk to. The interview took place at the school where she taught. Sabiha had married a rather conservative military engineer to comply with her father's

wishes. As she wanted to continue her university education, she refused all suitors until she was proposed to by a man who was not adverse to this idea–although he later used their children as an excuse for not allowing her to continue her studies. Her father had always treated her like a friend, but although she and her mother were close, her older sister and brother had received more attention and Sabiha was therefore deprived of much of the motherly kindness shown to her brother and sister. Her mother had full control over the children; she kept a close eye on them, decided what they should eat and discouraged them from reading non-academic books. She was not on good terms with her husband though they were cousins and knew each other well. She hated smoking but her husband smoked non-stop. (Sabiha later experienced the same problem with her husband.)

Sabiha grew up obedient and apprehensive. She was not allowed to visit friends, though her female friends could visit her at home. Even after her marriage she could not compensate for this as her husband was unsociable and used the children as an excuse for not allowing her to go out. Sabiha had full responsibility for the children, as her husband's military duties kept him away from home for all but a few days of every month. She had chosen to bring them up in her own way: she did not allow her parents to interfere, and told me that she treated all the children equally. When they were old enough to marry, she planned to consult them and to allow her daughters to get to know their future husbands first.

She did not believe in arranged marriages, feeling that a woman should try to get to know her partner first. She added that an ideal husband would be one with a good university education, who was religious and generous and helped his wife run the household and look after the children, if necessary. When her own husband was free or on holiday he did in fact help her. When he was away, however, he would not allow Sabiha to go out at all, not even to the shops. His nephew did the family's shopping, but even when he was not available Sabiha's husband still forbade her to go out. He told her that if she found she had no bread at home she must bake her own; if she did not have enough flour for bread she must bake cake. But under no circumstances was she to go out and buy it. Despite this she displayed a belief in the traditional role of a wife. She mentioned her uncle's wife, who had tolerated her alcoholic husband, helped him and cooked food for him, until eventually he gave up alcohol. When her brother-in-law's wife insisted her husband gave up alcohol, however, the problems mounted until they were almost divorced.

For Sabiha female emancipation was restricted to the idea that women should have access to a good education and should be able to mix with other people. They should have the same rights as Western women, except for being allowed to have sexual relations before marriage as this was against both religion and honour. Sabiha felt that young people should be encouraged to get married before they became sexually 'corrupt'. (By way of justification, she mentioned a neighbour who had set fire to her daughter and then pretended that it was an accident. Her son, who was a policeman, helped her in the affair. The reason was that the girl had become pregnant by a poor student.) Sabiha described her daily routine as follows:

> I wake up at 5 in the morning and prepare breakfast. I first wake up my younger son and feed him, then my daughter; the older children wake up later on and have their breakfast. I do some housework. At a quarter to 7 the nursery-school bus comes to pick up the children, but the eldest two go to my school so we go together. I make sure that the children are clean and tidy and have their books and belongings. The nursery bus delivers the children one hour after I get home. I wash and soak the rice early in the morning to be ready for

cooking in the afternoon. I even melt the oil so I don't have to spend long preparing the meal. Mind you, I cook the sauce for the whole week on Friday and freeze it, so all I do is get one out of the freezer a day in advance.

Anyway, after lunch I do the washing-up, clean up a bit and wash the clothes. Sometimes I can't do much work before the children go to bed, so I have to wait. I work very hard after that as I have to clean the house, dust the furniture, then prepare my teaching plan for the following day plus correcting my students' homework. As I told you, my husband works in the army, away from us, so he comes to stay with us only when he can get permission to do so, normally a few days a month; then he takes us out for visits or shopping. When he's away, I don't go anywhere at all. Anyway, he doesn't allow me to.

An Egyptian Comparison

It is interesting to compare the stories of Majida, Muna and Sabiha with that of a woman from Egypt. In *Woman and Neurosis*,[3] Nawal El Saadawi reported on her research into the root cause of women's neurotic illness. She discovered that those women she had chosen to study as neurotic cases were just ordinary women suffering from anxiety and social problems. The following is the story of Layla, one of her cases.

Layla worked in a ministry office, despite having a BA from an art college. It was a very simple clerical job which bore no relation to her college training. For a year, Layla had been going regularly to a psychiatrist, suffering from depression:

I wake up at 5 in the morning and get breakfast. My husband goes to work and my two oldest children go to school. I am left with the youngest. I carry him to my mother-in-law's, 2 km from us. Sometimes I take the bus, but I prefer walking to taking the baby in the crowded bus. My mother-in-law never welcomes him, but always complains to me about her health. She's had enough raising seven children. I leave her and take the bus to work.

Waiting for the bus and taking it to work normally takes me two hours. I feel so humiliated getting into a crowded bus where my body's squeezed in the middle of men–most of them are sexually frustrated–that I usually get off the bus and complete the trip on foot. When I arrive at work, I feel so tired, so tense and exhausted. My boss tells me off every day for being late, as I never arrive on time. Also, I take lots of days off . . . I looked for a servant or baby-minder to stay at home with the baby and help me with the cooking and the housework, but I couldn't find one. Nowadays servants demand a lot of money. One day, I told my husband I was going to leave work as I just couldn't manage. But we found we couldn't live on his money alone . . . I come back an hour before him, and despite my exhaustion, I start cooking. I get lunch ready for my husband and my two older children. When my husband goes to sleep, I go to my mother-in-law's to get the baby. At night I make supper for everyone and help my children with their homework. At 10 o'clock I lie down on my bed and I feel all the pain in the world. Nothing stops this pain but sleep.

My husband comes home very tired at 4 in the afternoon, eats and sleeps. In the evenings, he goes out. He tells me he's going to visit friends. When I ask him to stay in and help me, he argues with me and tells me he can't stay at home in the evening. I told him I didn't like it either. I wasn't only staying at home but I also had to do lots of work all on my own. He'd say, 'But all wives work at home in the evening and all husbands go out; this is life.' At the beginning of our marriage I used to feel some enjoyment in our sexual relations, but now, because of my exhaustion and nerves, I just cannot stand sex any more. But my husband gets so angry when I tell him I'm tired, he changes and goes out until the early hours of the morning. So I force myself to accept sex even though I'm so tired, which makes sexual intercourse another burden, physically and mentally, in my life.

I'm 32 now, but I don't feel young any more. I can't find any enjoyment in my life, in any part of it. I feel depressed now and then, and cannot sleep without sleeping pills. When the psychiatrist asked me about my sex life and I told him I hated it, he told me I'd become frigid and gave me pills and injections. I don't feel better. I'm much worse, particularly after I discovered that my husband loves another woman, and he leaves me every night and goes out to her. I'm so worried he might divorce me. I don't know what I'd do with the three children.

I can't bear living any more. I'm about to have a complete breakdown. I'm afraid I'll completely lose control and I have really scary thoughts, such as suicide. I sometimes think I'll find rest in death. Then I think about my children, as there's no one but me to look after them. My husband doesn't like looking after them, and always says it's a woman's job; men are never responsible for children, despite the fact that my husband's educated and a college graduate like me.

Layla, like others who appear in El Saadawi's book, is very similar to many of the Iraqi women I interviewed. They, too, showed symptoms of depression, as I discovered from their answers although, unlike El Saadawi, I did not set out to interview neurotic cases.

One of the issues El Saadawi examines in her study is the burden of housework. She found that many of the Egyptian women she studied, whether educated or not, and whether neurotic or not, received no help at all from their husbands. The picture was very similar among the Iraqi women.

Housework appears to be an important cause of depression. From their answers, many women revealed symptoms of depression when they said that they did not bother with their appearance any more, or felt indifferent about things or found themselves in a situation where they could not perform their daily tasks. Although housework is only one factor in such symptoms, it is clearly an important one and needs to be looked at in greater detail.

6
The Daily Grind: Housework

With the coming of the nuclear family, the burden of housework has increased tremendously, particularly for those women who are bringing up children and have a full-time job as well. Housework is a crucial issue, as it takes up most of a woman's day and energy. As will be seen, the Iraqi house requires a lot of upkeep and the meals that wives are expected to serve are elaborate and time-consuming. I was interested in the following issues. What is the role of socialization regarding housework for both sexes? Who does the housework in the natal family? In preparing girls for marriage, does the natal family train them to do the housework? Do women receive help from their husbands? Are servants available? And do modern gadgets reduce the burden? The chapter focuses on the situation of working women, as in having a home to run as well as an outside job, they inevitably face extra problems.

The Iraqi House and its Upkeep
The average urban Iraqi dwelling consists of two floors with a roof, where people sleep in the summer. On the ground floor, the hall is usually used as a gathering place for the family, while a second room is used for visitors, with the finest furniture, the

family antiques and the best carpet. In April people often hire professionals to clean their carpets, which are then rolled up and put aside until November, as carpets add unnecessary warmth to the hot Iraqi summer. Vacuum cleaners and carpet sweepers have now become popular, but brooms made of palm leaves are still used to clean carpets in winter. The floors are usually made of stone tiles, which must be washed by hand in summer. Because so much dust blows in from the desert on the western edge of Iraq, the floors may need daily washing.

Most kitchens are similar to those in the West. Though a few people still use an old-style cooker which burns paraffin oil, the majority cook by gas. People have to buy gas cylinders from petrol stations or have them delivered as there is no piped gas supply. Bedrooms are also organized like those in the West. However, eiderdowns are still generally used as bed covers instead of duvets, which have only recently been introduced to Iraq. The eiderdown covers are sewn sheets, which have to be unstitched when they need washing. The stitching and unstitching process is therefore repeated frequently, and is a time-consuming chore.

In general, cleaning rituals can be seen as an important part of cultural behaviour–Islam places a high value on cleanliness. The entire house, especially the visitors' room, is expected to be clean. This cultural requirement is made more demanding by the all-pervasive dust; walls, furniture and pictures must be dusted at least once a week. Untidiness could be embarrassing if visitors drop in without warning. This places a significant burden on the housewife, compared to her Western counterpart, particularly if she is a working woman.

The Iraqi Meal
Lunch is the main daily meal in the Iraqi household. It usually consists of meat with vegetable sauce and rice, and can take up to

two hours to prepare. Women usually cook more than is needed in order to be prepared for the unexpected visitor. For guests women cook a number of different dishes; they also cook more than needed as a sign of hospitality. Traditional Arab hospitality and the concern for food[1] make it necessary to prepare several dishes rather than one only, as is generally the case in the West.

In *The Guests of the Sheik*, Elizabeth Fernea described the dinner to which she invited Sheik Hamid. She listed what she had to prepare, doing it the Iraqi way, like the people in the village of el-Nahra, who 'wanted to provide enough food to honour the sheik in traditional fashion'. Here is Fernea's menu:

Chicken and noodle soup
Grilled kebabs, beef in spiced tomato sauce
Lamb cooked with beans and onions and fresh dill
2 whole roast chickens; 3 fried chickens, American style
Caucasian rice (with raisins, almonds, onions, chicken livers, butter and saffron)
Eggplant in meat sauce, sliced tomato salad
Yogurt, *khubuz* (flat wheat bread), homemade Western bread
Butter and jam
Strawberry jelly, caramel custard, sponge cake
Cookies, fresh fruit (bananas and oranges)
Tea and coffee.[2]

What Fernea had to prepare for the sheik in 1965 is more or less typical of what many Iraqi women still have to prepare for their ordinary guests who are invited for a meal.

Other Household Jobs
Until the early 1980s, when washing machines became widely available and popular, Iraqi women usually did their washing in a large metal tub. The washing is normally done on the bathroom

floor, which has a hole in it to drain the water away; or in old houses, the side garden or courtyard might be used. It involves three washes and three rinses, the first to remove dust and the next two with washing powder.

Clothes are normally dried on a washing line on the roof, to keep them away from the eyes of inquisitive neighbours. It would be particularly shameful for women's underwear to be seen. This custom often necessitates a woman climbing two long flights of stairs to take clothes up to the roof, rather than using a line in the garden. During the long hot season, which lasts more than seven months, daily washing and ironing is essential. In addition, winter clothes must be cleaned and packed away with moth balls in April and unpacked and aired to use again in November (the same process is repeated for summer clothes, but without the moth balls).

In the summer there are extra jobs for women: cleaning the roof, taking the beds inside each morning and putting them out again in the evening. Other jobs include washing down the balconies and sometimes watering the garden every evening, as the family usually sits outside or eats there, where it is cooler.

It will be apparent from the foregoing (and from the daily routines of Majida, Muna and Sabiha in Chapter 5) that a large proportion of women's time is spent on housework. I was interested to discover whether they receive help from their husbands, as they are one of the possible sources of support.

Husbands and Housework

Housework has always been considered a woman's duty. Men and women are socialized to believe and practise this in everyday life–a man doing the housework would be looked down on and seen as acting like a woman. Husbands' attitudes have not changed with the transition from the traditional to the nuclear family, even though the double burden of running a house and working outside the home are too heavy for one person to carry. For the women I met, an important problem was society's expectation that they should take full responsibility for the housework. Thus while they see themselves as wholly responsible, the burden is too great for them to stay in control. They do not know what to do. Since they are not merely overworked but also puzzled, they start looking at their lives in terms of problems and spend a great deal of time complaining.

Not one of the women I interviewed had a husband who helped with the housework. When I asked what kind of tasks would have been acceptable if their husband had been willing to help, I was told that 'dirty' jobs would be excluded. Most of the housework comes under this category, starting with sweeping the floor and ending with washing the dishes, so even if the husbands had been willing to help, there would have been no suitable jobs for them to do.

Men do not help with cleaning, dusting, scrubbing floors, changing the baby, washing clothes or doing the washing up. Most husbands gave no help at all:

He never helps. Sometimes I ask him to, but he says that women are women and men are men. (*Shada*)

He doesn't help; he grew up like that. Also his mother lives with us. If I miss out something she'd do it. (*Madiha*)

He hardly helps me at all.
Q: What kind of housework would you like to see him helping with?
A: I wouldn't expect him to do everything. As a matter of fact, he doesn't even do some of the jobs that are expected of men. (*Suha*)

He helps with the carpets. In the garden, there are quite a few things he can help with if he wants to, such as hanging his clothes out after he changes, for instance, but to make him do that, I have to remind him every day. I always think it's easier for me to do it myself. (*Haifa*)

Suha and Haifa's comments are interesting as they show that certain domestic tasks are regarded as 'men's work' (even though the women would hesitate to ask their husband for help if he did not offer). These tasks include moving heavy furniture, buying gas cylinders, gardening and repairing electrical faults. In addition, most husbands help with removing the carpets in April and relaying them in November. As the carpets normally used in the Iraqi household need several people to handle them, it would be impossible for women to do this job alone. In other words, if it is physically possible for a job to be done by women on their own, men are not expected to help.

A few husbands gave limited help on rare occasions:

On Friday [the weekend holiday in Iraq] he makes the salad, sometimes. (*Samar*)

Yes, for example, if he sees me cooking and the baby cries, so I have to run and pick him up, he'll check the food and switch the cooker off if needed. (*Labiba*)

Some husbands also help when the wife is ill (in this instance, they are not seen as losing face by doing 'women's work'). A woman will often return to her parents' home in case of sickness, however, or neighbours, friends and relatives may step in to help if her family lives far away or cannot offer support.[3] Husbands frequently disapprove of the wife receiving help from her natal family: they want to limit this dependency so that their wife becomes more submissive. They may also wish to avoid being obliged to the wife's family–this would give them less freedom to deal with her harshly.

The deepest conflict over housework, however, arises not between the woman and her husband, but within the woman herself. The women I spoke to appeared to be confused about what they wanted. On the one hand, they needed help, whether from their husband or someone else, and a husband seems to be the only one who can give such help within the nuclear family. On the other hand, they were determined not to go against tradition by asking men to help. This conflict is illustrated in the following statements:

He does help when he finds it absolutely necessary. I never ask him, I don't know why. Maybe I think that I would humiliate him and also humiliate myself, too, as housework isn't for men. (*Maisoon*)

He helps with little things like making salads . . . I don't really like to see him doing any housework. It's not a man's job, is it? (*Ibtihal*)

He does some work. For example, he'd get breakfast. He'd prepare an appetiser. He helps me laying and removing the carpets. He refuses to clean the house but on the other hand I want him to maintain his status at home; I don't want him to do any of the house cleaning. (*Nazira*)

Yes, he helps . . . If I'm ill he cooks and buys food and gives it to the children. I personally wouldn't like it if he cleaned the house. That's shameful, you know. (*Labiba*)

He helps sometimes, with a few things, but I don't want him to do the menial jobs anyway. (*Fadwa*)

Occasionally he helps but neither he nor I expect him to sweep and clean the house. He thinks that a man's personality is threatened if he does these things at home and I don't want him to think that. So I don't want him to even try these jobs. (*Hala*)

Yes, he always helps . . . He collects the rubbish bag and takes it outside at night–but only because we live on the main street and he doesn't want people to see me doing it. He also makes the salad. I don't accept his help cleaning the house. I started doing what he wanted as soon as we got married and he got used to it. Women who had more experience would probably cope better with their husbands; from the beginning they act differently with them, and they make them used to that and accept it. But to tell you the truth, I don't think it's nice to see a man doing housework anyway. (*Ansam*)

Time and again, the same preoccupation was revealed: women are anxious not to 'humiliate' their husband by seeing him do the dirty housework. For a woman, however, housework is not considered humiliating. While executive women are aware of the importance of equality between the sexes and believe in shared responsibility between husbands and wives, they nevertheless appear to be very conscious of their husband's or society's reaction. Even if a woman holds a high post, she does not believe this makes her her husband's equal. If a woman tries to make a man do the housework, that will be taken to mean that she is 'wearing the trousers' and thus humiliating him; this will humiliate her too, for being married to such a man.

A woman may be educated and have a responsible position at work, but the influence of socialization and traditional beliefs remains strong:

He never helps and I never ask him to. I don't know why.

Maybe because this was unusual and I didn't see my father or brother doing the housework. I always felt it was my duty to do it, and I wouldn't want him or other people to think that just because I have an important position I make my husband do the housework. (*Nada*)

He would only help me if it was really necessary and only if we were alone at home, I mean, if there were no visitors or in-laws around. He mainly helps with the big jobs such as taking away the carpets, preparing for the summer. (*Huda*)

Huda's point is of particular importance: she would accept help 'only if we were alone at home'. Even if men wanted to help with the housework, they would not do so if other people were around in order to 'avoid humiliation'. For those living with the in-laws, particularly the husband's family, the situation is even worse:

Well, even if he were willing to help–and I wouldn't mind some help–he couldn't anyway, as we're living with my parents. (*Siham*)

In some cases, the husband not only refuses to help around the house but it bothers him if his wife does the housework while he is around:

He doesn't help, and I don't expect him to, but the thing is, he doesn't allow me to do it if he's at home; it bothers him a lot. He usually says, 'The house will fall apart because you clean it so much. Can't you do it when I'm out? Do you have to bother me like this whenever I come home?' (*Jamila*)

Several women criticized their husband's behaviour, in different ways, but making the same general point. Although pouring tea was clearly the easiest thing in the world to do, a common complaint was that the man would not do it himself:

> My husband never helps with the housework. For example, if he's sitting having breakfast and I'm doing the washing, he'll call me to pour him a cup of tea even though the teapot is right next to him. (*Fawzia*)

> He doesn't help at all. I even have to pour his tea for him. (*Khadija*)

Support from the husband is thus not taken for granted in Iraq, as it often is in the West. Owing to the weaker family ties, Western couples tend to rely on each other more and will share both chores and pleasures. In Iraq, each partner tends to spend time with members of their own natal family. Elderly couples lead their lives almost separate from each other.

Gadgets and Servants
Since Iraqi women cannot expect help from their husbands, I wondered whether their burden might be lightened by household gadgets or servants. I was also interested in discovering whether differences in social class and educational level are factors here.

It has become very difficult to distinguish class in Iraqi society. Middle-class status might tend to suggest the availability in the home of more modern equipment to lighten the burden of housework. From what the women told me, however, it appears that many illiterate women–theoretically more likely to be working class–have much more modern equipment than, for example, a teacher. The average Iraqi kitchen has an oven, refrigerator and freezer, and quite possibly a dishwasher, microwave oven and food processor. Having all this equipment does not necessarily reduce the amount of work. Not all foodstuffs are readily available (at the time I conducted the interviews, subsidized imported meat could only be bought once or twice a month). As a result, shop-size freezers have recently become popular in the home and women are expected to cook and freeze large quantities of food as soon as they are purchased. They are also expected to bake different types of cake, pastry, bread, and so on–these used to be bought from shops before modern kitchen appliances became available.

The changing class structure has also affected the availability of servants. Only three of the women I spoke to had domestic help for a few hours a week. Although these women were wealthy, they were not necessarily middle class. This is a major change from twenty years ago. Up to the 1960s all educated working women, as well as many from the middle class, could afford to employ servants in the home. The increases in oil revenues, however, opened up many job opportunities; large numbers of servants gave up their domestic jobs to work in the state sector, where they could earn more money and enjoy higher social status. As a result, families could only employ servants if they were willing to offer salaries that were competitive with government wages. Nowadays a domestic servant may be earning more money than a bank employee with a university degree. Before the increase in oil revenues, the servant's wages would have been no more than 20% of the bank employee's salary.

Employing servants thus became a rarity, as they were difficult to find. Foreign servants tended not to stay long; the work attracted women who wanted to make money, but not to settle. They could earn a lot in a short period of time and then leave. Such behaviour was not popular with Iraqi families; while a foreign woman might charge less, a family wished to know their servant well, and preferred to find a moral, hard-working Iraqi woman who would remain with the family for a long time, thus saving the time and effort of finding new servants. However, there are few such women left nowadays.

The lack of resources available within the nuclear family creates another problem in relation to child-bearing and child-rearing. The loss of the traditional female support network within the extended family has not been compensated for by sufficient nurseries or child-minders. Newborn babies represent a new responsibility and an additional burden rather than joy for the mother, particularly if she is working. I was anxious to discover why working mothers are keen to keep their jobs despite their exhausting life-style.

Working Mothers

In many societies, the majority of wives are full-time housewives, and many married women leave their jobs after the birth of their first child. Some return to work after the children start school and others take part-time jobs once their children are no longer infants. The situation in Iraq is very different. The majority of young mothers with newborn babies carry on working; some take only the six weeks' leave for which they get full pay, but many take six months with half pay.[4] If the mother does return to work, she places the baby under the care of in-laws, relatives, friends or neighbours. In other cases the baby will go to a nursery, if one is available in the area. In the past, servants or child-minders would be employed to care for babies, but this is rapidly disappearing with their soaring wages.

There are many reasons why women return to work. For example:

> Although it's hard enough to do the housework, look after the children, plus working outside, I find going out to work a relief. When I'm at home in the holidays I hardly bother to change or wear make-up. These things cheer you up sometimes. I feel more alive when I go out to work. (*Muna*)

When I'm at home I feel the housework is never done. It's always waiting for me. At least when I'm working I forget about it. I get fed up with the children always crying and wanting things. (*Rafida*)

There are a number of other reasons why women carry on working. First and perhaps most important is the inflexibility of the job system itself. Although jobs are available it is not officially acceptable to leave a job and return to it freely, so a woman may return to work quickly for financial reasons, particularly if she knows that going back to the same job will not be easy after the prolonged leave. Of course, others wish to return to work as a means of 'running away from home', which tends to represent continuous housework as Muna and Rafida–among others– indicated. Meeting other people is also important to women and the loss of their jobs makes that more difficult. Working women felt it helped greatly to communicate with other people as they had difficulties communicating with their husband at home (see Chapter 4). Working was even more important to those women who were not normally free to go out, as it represented some freedom for them.

The working women I interviewed did not appear to enjoy any better status for having a job, nor did they have much job satisfaction. Although paid work gives a woman some independence and a feeling of being useful, it should also build her self-confidence. However, when life at home is so exhausting because of housework, and personal problems become paramount, the job is less valuable and in fact a woman might be happier as a housewife.

'Rewards' for Housework

In her acclaimed work, *The Sociology of Housework*, Ann Oakley discusses the important notion of rewards for housework:

The housewife receives no wage for the work. Rewards of a more subtle kind thus have to be substituted. The husband is one potentially appreciative figure in the housewife's landscape–but does he play this role effectively?[5]

None of the women she interviewed indicated that their husband's comments were 'a source of personal reward for doing housework'.

I found exactly the same situation among the Iraqi women I spoke to: the majority mentioned neither rewards nor appreciation. They seemed to be complaining not only about the lack of help with housework but also about not being rewarded:

When I cook a nice meal for him, which usually takes hours of preparation–you know how long our food takes to cook–of course, I'd like him to comment on it. Any nice word would make me forget I was tired, or even if he said nothing I wouldn't mind either, but instead he says things like, 'You deliberately cook this food. You know I like it very much and will eat a lot of it; you're just doing it to make me fat.' Of course, if I didn't cook what he liked, he'd make a real fuss. (*Muna*)

Training for Domesticity

Because girls are socialized to believe that their main role in life is that of housewife and mother, it is not surprising that they believe housework is solely their responsibility. They are taught that a good housewife keeps the house clean and tidy, cooks good meals, and manages everything to ensure the comfort and happiness of her husband and children. Socialization, which can be seen as an extended process of preparing girls from an early age to fulfil such roles, involves the family, schools and the media. In reality, however, Iraqi girls are ill prepared for domesticity and there is no actual training for it. If the family is rich, servants do the housework under the mother's supervision and girls grow up knowing nothing about it. If the family cannot afford servants, the oldest sister will be well trained–but mainly because the mother needs a helping hand, rather than in any attempt to teach the girl household skills which might help her when she gets married. Many unmarried girls, even in poor families, do not have to do the housework if there are enough women in the household to perform these duties.

Many of the women I met came from large families with several children, and the oldest sister played the role of mother, looking after the younger ones. Several women spoke of their elder sister as one would about one's mother. Some of the housewives told me they were registered to go to school, but had to leave because their mother needed them to help with the housework, while their younger sisters continued at school. It is interesting that the only difference between the women I interviewed and their daughters' generation regarding education and housework is that the latter's schooling was not interrupted to help their mother with the housework. Despite the fact that this is a positive aspect for the new generation, such a change of attitude (brought about by modernization) implies again that women are now deprived of another source of help in the home without an alternative being available.

A 1956 study on Iraqi women also found that girls were unprepared for housework. Although some thirty years have now elapsed, the training for girls has hardly changed; they are still unprepared for housework despite the generally accepted social belief that they are socialized to fill the role of housewives and mothers.[6]

When describing their mother's relationship with their father, many women stated that their mothers were excellent housewives and cooks; this was often in the context of a father's unkind treatment of a mother. They implied that there was often no reason for this mistreatment as their mothers were first-rate housewives, implying that they had all the 'right' qualities to ensure their husband's respect. The women in the 1956 study also mentioned that their mothers worked hard at home. This demonstrates how deep-rooted is the ideology of being a good housewife. The aim of all this housework, then, is to achieve a better marriage and a better, loving husband. At the same time, most of today's women have no preparation for those domestic tasks which would make them, like their mothers, 'excellent housewives and excellent cooks'. The result is that the young wives spend the first months of their marriages trying to master household skills; during this time they are worried and anxious as they do not feel they are performing adequately. (This is the same period that Western culture tends to see as the most blissful and problem-free.)

Women do the housework, bear and bring up the children and serve their husband, even if they are working outside the home doing a similar job to their husband. Despite this burden, they are considered to be weaker creatures than men, thus complying with so-called 'feminine behaviour':

> We used to regard my father as if he was a king and we were his subjects. This is how my mother behaved and I do exactly the same with my husband. The moment I get back from school I do the washing up and I cook, clean and do the ironing. Sometimes at school we talk about how tired we are all the time, but what's the alternative?, the work has to be done. (*Salwa*)

Although housework occupies a major part of Iraqi women's time, the question remains as to whether it also occupies their mind. Most women, particularly those who were better educated, felt that whatever problems they had in general, housework would make them even worse. Only a few women found some satisfaction in their daily chores.

When discussing a girl prior to arranging a marriage, people will consider her family background, appearance, age, and perhaps her education and job. Her ability to do housework comes at the bottom of the list. Only sewing or knitting might be mentioned, as people tend to believe that if the girl does not know anything about housework, it means she was well looked after by her family, that she was loved by them and other people served her. Many of the women I met reflected their pride at never having done the housework before marriage. This dramatic change at marriage could explain their resentment of it. Their inexperience also made their mothers worry about them, as they wondered how they would cope. Many indicated that their parental family helped with the housework or cooking after marriage. The following is a typical example:

My family used to spoil me when I was still at home. My husband started treating me just the opposite. He objected when my family did the cooking for us when we first married. He lost his temper because I didn't know how to cook special dishes. I've often arrived at places late because I've been preparing food for him. He doesn't do anything at home. I even have to switch on the radio for him. Sometimes when I'm really ill, he still asks me to fetch him a glass of water or switch the television on.
Q: If he was willing to help, would you let him?
A: That would be a dream. The only thing he does is wash his car, go into the garden and make the carpet dirty. (*Fatima*)

In conclusion, here as in other areas Iraqi women are in the unfortunate position of having adopted the worst of both worlds. They have to some extent lost the supportive shared life of the traditional household. But although they now live in the privacy of the nuclear family, they have not yet achieved the advantages of a marriage in which not only recreation but also housework is shared.

7
Independence:
Is Divorce a Solution?

Independence within Marriage

Although education, work and modernization have introduced
the notion of independence, the strong process of socialization
ensures that women hold fast to traditional social values. This
chapter examines the issue of women's dependency in Iraq, with
special reference to their status within marriage and their
attitudes towards ending a marriage. I wanted to discover how far
women are dependent on their natal family even after their
marriage and how far they have to accept an unhappy marriage or
a violent husband to avoid being labelled 'divorced'.

Chapter 1 showed how the process of socializing girls in Iraqi
society shapes them as dependent beings: they are identified only
as someone's daughter, sister, wife or even mother. They are not
taught to think, only to respond emotionally, thus leaving other
family members to make decisions for them while remaining
politically harmless themselves. It may be true that Iraqi women
are sentimental and emotional, but this is due to their limited
social space and to the process of socialization, which encourages
the characteristics that are considered feminine. Due to their
upbringing many women see such characteristics as natural
female attributes.

The women's answers revealed that most of them were raised to be dependent first on their family and then, after marriage, on their husband and (natal) family. In order to evaluate how they viewed their independence, I asked a series of questions ranging from, 'Have you ever wished you'd been born a boy?' to, 'Have you ever regretted being married?' Answers to the first question revealed some of the women's most private wishes:

I used to be naughty when I was little and behaved like a boy. People used to say that I was masculine. I wished I'd been born a boy because whatever I did they said, 'You're a girl, don't do that.' (*Fatin*)

I've always wished I was a boy, ever since I was a little girl. I used to wear boys' clothes and play their games. I love the freedom that boys have. Before puberty, they didn't mind. They allowed me to do those things, but since then I haven't felt free. Our society is so hard on women. (*Siham*)

Yes, of course I wanted to be a boy–I'd have been free to go and visit my brothers. And all this tiredness and suffering would be lifted from my shoulders. (*Jamila*)

More than half of the women said they wished they had been born a boy. Many related their wish to the oppression women suffer in society:

On many occasions I've wished I wasn't a woman, because they're oppressed in this society and denied their rights. Now I wish that I had a baby boy rather than a girl for the same reason. (*Hajir*)

Fadwa explained in some detail the privileges enjoyed by men:

Men are allowed to do so many things that women are deprived of. They don't have to worry about their appearance, while women have to wear tight, uncomfortable garments such as bras, corsets and high-heeled shoes. Men's hair is short and easy to take care of. They can choose who they want to marry and when to get married. If a woman dies, her husband wears a black tie for a few days and then gets married again as soon as possible, while a widow has to wear black clothes for years in mourning for her husband and her chances of remarriage are very slim. Men don't get pregnant and don't have periods. They're supported by society, God and the law.

I think a man can express his opinions freely and behave as he pleases. He doesn't have to keep things to himself and can free his mind from any oppressed ideas and problems. (*Suha*)

The most important reasons the women gave for wanting to be male were related to the freedom and experience men enjoy. While freedom could bring independence for women it would also bring shame, so they only want freedom if they could at the same time become male:

If I were a man I'd be able to make decisions. (*Sabiha*)

I love the freedom boys have. (*Siham*)

We don't have the power to do anything. (*Iqbal*)

My second question was, 'Do you believe that a woman with a strong personality has a better marriage? If not, why not?' The answers revealed that most of the women embodied the traditional submissiveness expected of females in their mode of thinking. The majority felt that a woman with a strong personality would have an unsuccessful marriage, while an obedient woman had a chance of a successful one. It is significant that while most of them spoke of being obedient, their answers throughout the interviews suggested that rather than having a successful marriage, theirs was problem-ridden. Here are some examples of their answers:

> A woman with a strong personality would be very tired mentally or generally over-stressed as a wife. I think the subordinate ones are much more successful. (*Jamila*)

> Obedience is much better. (*Rahima*)

> In Iraq, obedience is better. A strong woman can cause conflict with her husband as she tends to impose her views and I don't think there's a man who accepts these things. (*Sabiha*)

In seeing the obedient woman as happier than the more independent-minded one, they were seeing the obedient woman as one who sacrifices normal ambitions; in order to prevent any conflict and problems with her husband, she devotes herself entirely to him and the children. As a result she neglects herself and her needs. The extent of her sacrifices, however, depends on how strongly she has been socialized to fulfil her role. Women who are educated and manage to get jobs learn to be analytical; they gain some self-confidence and independence. Most of all, they begin to question and reject the husband's attitude at home, which creates conflict between them. This results in a very stressful situation which more submissive women do not experience. Although work also has positive aspects for women and adds to the family income, the life-style involved can become a trap unless the husband can modify his attitudes to accommodate his wife's needs. Having a job does not seem to play a major role in an Iraqi woman's life; the responses of the working women I spoke to differed little from those of the illiterate housewives.

We cannot ignore the changes brought by education, which help professional women see their lives from a different perspective; despite these changes, most of the women still viewed obedience as better than a strong personality. One respondent did say that a stronger woman would do better, but she did not really believe it. Had her answers been given in a questionnaire, I would have believed her, but as I was speaking to her face-to-face, I knew from her expression and tone of voice that she was being sarcastic:

> I think a strong woman is more successful in life. These days things are the opposite to what they should be. A strong woman can do what she likes, go out and return as she wishes without having permission from her husband. (*Muna*)

Thus even the woman whose answer was somewhat sarcastic reflected the ambivalence that results from changing standards. By saying, 'These days things are the opposite to what they should be', Muna meant that although there are some women with strong personalities who have a successful marriage, this is wrong as it does not fit into the traditional pattern.

One of the problems related to independence for Iraqi women is the price they have to pay, primarily in terms of their future husband. A man will never ask for a woman's hand in marriage if he finds out that she is independent. The great majority of women, in all three categories, stated that obedient women were more successful in life. This is not necessarily because they believe this or accept this role for women, but only because they know that men prefer obedient women and so they adopt this attitude in order to please men:

Iraqi men prefer obedient women. (*Fatin*)

Obedience is better; a strong woman can cause conflict between herself and her husband. (*Sabiha*)

If a woman isn't obedient she would only harm herself. (*Khadija*)

This suggests that a woman has only two choices: to have a 'normal' life with marriage and children or to drive men away from her. The women seemed to draw a sharp line separating dependent, married women from independent, unmarried women.

In trying to discover whether the women were satisfied with their marriage or not, I asked, 'Have you ever regretted being married?' Some gave casual short answers:

I regretted the idea in the first place. (*Fawzia*)

Yes, on many occasions I regret it. (*Feryal*)

I regret it when I see him drinking heavily or when he quarrels with me or when I get fed up with my children, but these things don't happen every day. (*Siham*)

Yes, I always feel that. (*Bahira*)

Yes, at the beginning of our marriage he was cruel and misunderstood me. (*Hala*)

Others were more emphatic:

Yes, I've wasted part of my life with a stupid man who can't keep a secret and who has no values whether religious or social. He's not to be trusted. (*Fadwa*)

Yes, they destroyed me in this marriage, but I must say that on the whole it's better than living with my family. I was under tremendous pressure when I was living with them. If someone came to visit, we had to hide until they left. (*Nazhat*)

Although the women's comments were primarily negative, it should be noted that many of their husbands had the qualities which earned them respect in the eyes of society as a whole, such as drive, initiative and intelligence, as witnessed by the kinds of responsible and demanding jobs many of them held. Most of the comments were related to the wife's personal relationship with her husband rather than to the qualities the men had as fathers or sons, workers or citizens. Since men evidently need not worry what their wives think of them, they do not have to behave and show their good sides as husbands.

Sabiha pointed out reasons to regret her marriage:

Yes, sometimes I feel I'm oppressed and exhausted. I have children but my husband's in the army so he's always away. The responsibility is on my shoulders in addition to the other restrictions. That's life and I have to accept it.

Jamila said:

I sometimes regret my marriage and I wish I'd married a relative who at least knows me. Then, if he swore at me the swearing would be against his own family. If he'd been a cousin of mine, we wouldn't have lacked anything. I married an outsider who swears at me, insults me and is ill-mannered at home. I'm extremely sorry and regret my marriage.

She highlighted the importance of blood relations in protecting one's honour and the family's expectations for such a marriage by saying, 'If he swore at me the swearing would be against his own family.' If only she had been more independent-minded, she would have been able to protect herself against his swearing without bringing in her family.

Very few of the women did not regret being married; a handful saw no point in having regrets. The majority made their feelings very clear. The next question, however, revealed an interesting paradox. I asked, 'If you were given the chance again, would you choose the same life and the same man? If not, what would you have done?' Surprisingly, most women said they would choose the same man again (although a few qualified this by adding, somewhat hesitantly, 'if he was a different man'). This can be explained in terms of social expectations. It is not honourable for a woman to think about an alternative to her husband; she is meant to have only one man throughout her life. To admit an interest in another man, even in the imagination, would be immodest and shameful. Also because women believe in fate, they say 'it is written' (*maktub*) for them to marry this man; it is all meant to be and they should accept it. Who knows?, some told me, another man could be worse.

Of the few women who would have chosen the same man, but with certain conditions, Sabiha and Amina were typical:

I would have chosen the same man, but I would expect him to give me more freedom to purchase what I need and to allow me to go out freely. (*Sabiha*)

I would have chosen the same man but I would either have changed him or myself. He took advantage of me. Now it's too late to change, he's used to me like this. It's no use pretending. (*Amina*)

Rafida's answer was different. She would have liked different qualities in her husband, but she pointed out the social restrictions on girls which result in their not having the freedom to meet and get to know the man before marriage. At present, the man puts on an act in front of the woman he proposes to marry, thus hiding his real personality and making it hard for the girl to choose a partner:

Yes, I would have chosen the same man but with different qualities, better than the present ones. But the problem is, how would I know what the truth was? I might have a man who acts as if he's loving and caring until I get married and then it would be too late, wouldn't it? (*Rafida*)

Lutfia and Samar related their choice of partner to their age and way of thinking before marriage:

I would have chosen the same man had I been asked during the same stage of my life. It might be different if I was younger. (*Lutfia*)

I'd have done the same thing if I had the same mentality and not my present mentality. (*Samar*)

Wafaa, in contrast, showed total submission to her family's choice:

I can't choose another man.

The following are some of the negative answers to my question:

No, I wish I hadn't met him at all. (*Iqbal*)

No, of course I wouldn't have chosen the same man. I've been really tormented. (*Sahira*)

I wouldn't have chosen any man. Now, I advise my nieces to work for university degrees and good jobs rather than being ambitious about marriage and looking for men. Of course, my sister thinks I'm dissuading her daughters from marriage. (*Jamila*)

Most of the women said they had major problems in their marriage and many wished they had never married at all. Nearly all of them would choose a different man if this did not involve social disapproval. This indicates that most of their marriages were not successful.

The next issue I addressed was whether an unhappy marriage could be improved. Unfortunately there seems to be little communication between husband and wife:

We sometimes sit down to talk, but he shouts at me and the kids, so we leave him alone. (*Labiba*)

In spite of having suffered a great deal of oppression, Labiba told me:

I would have chosen the same man. We [her and her natal family] want only one man. If something happened to him I'd kill myself.

She meant that she came from an honourable family whose women would know only one man. Labiba's story is interesting, and it is instructive to look in detail at her description of her relationship with her husband, which contains features common to many marital relationships in Iraq:

I always think about how miserable I am with him and how badly he treats me and my daughters. I constantly think about trying to change his behaviour towards me, but I don't get anywhere . . .

I wish God could change my husband's behaviour. I wish we could have our own house and decent furniture . . .

He beats me whenever he feels angry or something. I always forgive him. I say he's 'a tent over my head'. I say, 'Where can I go?' I have no parents. Even my uncle is impossible.

My husband spends all his money on *arak* [a strong alcoholic drink]. In the past when racing was legal, he used to gamble all the time. Then he drank, particularly when he lost. Then he'd come home and give us hell. He doesn't give us enough money for housekeeping.

He told me about an engineer who works with him. She's a 22-year-old widow and as he's a bus driver for the office she works in, he gives her a lift to work and back every day. He said she loves him, and consulted me about marrying her. I said 'Go ahead,' but he said he didn't want us to live together. He would pay me and the children but would live with her. She was married for only one year and has no children; her husband was killed fighting in the war with Iran. Also she's very well off . . . He's making my life hell. If he wants to do it, he'll do it anyway, so what's the point in arguing? He said I should go and see her. She's so modern and her perfume and make-up are beautiful. I must say I don't use any make-up because I'm often unwell and don't feel in the right mood . . . He's waiting to settle everything with us first. Then he'll ask for her hand . . .

Q: How do you know she's beautiful?

He said so, but I also saw her myself. I was sweeping outside our house one day when I saw him driving the office bus. He slowed down when he saw me but didn't wave or anything. He told me later that the lady in the bus was 'her' and he told her that this was his house and she'd asked if I was his mother. She was the only one left in the bus. I must admit she's very pretty and young.

How can we explain this situation? Did Labiba's husband want to hurt her feelings? Or was he merely an excellent example of the over-confidence Iraqi men have in general? This man came from a working-class background and had only four years of schooling, while his passenger was a middle-class engineer with seventeen years of schooling. He was 47 years old and a father of seven children, while she was 22 and had no children. He had a wife, while she was a widow. She was well off while he was quite poor. Clearly they were not an appropriate match. His over-confidence, however, had led to much anxiety for everyone involved. This case indicates very clearly how men view women who have been 'used before' or in other words are not virgins. Not only did he imagine that this young widow loved him; he had also decided to marry her and had discussed the matter with his wife, though he did not seem to have discussed it with the woman in question.

Taking such stories into account, why do women do nothing about their situation? When it is as bad as Labiba's, for example, what is their attitude to change? Has divorce ever occurred to them as an alternative?

Ending a Marriage
Marriage is highly valued in Iraqi society, to the extent that it is considered to be the main aim in life. In such a culture, divorce can lower a woman's status to the point that she will have most doors shut in her face, whether that be professional opportunities or the loss of her women friends; most husbands would not approve of their wife's friendship with a divorced woman. Above all, a second marriage is almost out of the question unless a woman

is prepared to marry someone with a much lower standard, as in the case of Labiba's husband above.

It has been noted that:

> In the Middle East, remarriage of widows, and more particularly of divorcees, is neither expected nor socially approved. Among other considerations, the high value placed on virginity at marriage automatically excludes previously married women from the ranks of 'desired' mates.[1]

The fearful consequences of divorce are therefore an issue in Iraq, where marriage is so highly valued. It accounts for the existence of many unhappy marriages and women trying to keep them alive. Women face a dreadful dilemma because while they struggle to make their marriage work, as can be seen from the interviews, they live in a permanent state of unhappiness as a result.

When girls are brought up to be imaginative, sentimental and emotional, they expect their husbands to treat them with affection. This is particularly true, given the high value society places on marriage and the way women see it as the main aim in life. This expectation, as is evident from the women's replies, was almost universally unfulfilled. Men cannot understand their wife's needs as they are not socialized to do so. Moreover, their upbringing teaches them to be tough and express no emotion, as described in Chapter 1.

Given this situation, what is the process of divorce like in Iraq? Is it a reasonable option for a woman in an unhappy marriage? The Quran states, 'Of all the lawful things, divorce is the most disliked in the eyes of God'–it is lawful, however. Statistics show that divorce is filed mainly by the husband. Despite the fact that it is an easy procedure in Muslim societies, the divorce rate in Iraq is low compared with that in more developed countries where the law and religion are often more restrictive.

The low status of divorced women in Iraqi society, coupled with the lack of rights, explains women's attitudes towards divorce. None of those I spoke to saw it as a solution to marital problems. They also felt that a divorcee would find it very hard to adjust in society. Their attitude was that a woman should be patient and make sacrifices, thus trying to make the marriage successful. The most extreme case was Nabiha, whose husband had divorced her and remarried:

> I was dressed in black for three years after my divorce. I was always sad and miserable during that time because my dignity was hurt.

For most women, divorce was out of the question:

> Divorce has never occurred to me and I never ever consider it as a solution. (*Samar*)

> God forbid! I don't want to approve of divorce. (*Labiba*)

> I don't believe in divorce. I think problems can be solved between a woman and her husband, but that depends on the woman, her nature and personality.
> *Q*: Why does that depend on the woman?
> *A*: I'm educated and a politician with a responsible position but with my husband I have to be down-to-earth and understanding. I should adapt to his habits and our marriage. I should make him happy.
> *Q*: Why do *you* have to adapt and not him?
> *A*: In my experience, the woman should adapt to fulfil her happiness. Divorce is not a solution. A woman can adapt to the man. (*Hala*)

Bint al-halal tusber o tet-hamal is an Iraqi saying which could be translated as, 'A girl who comes from a good family can cope with any situation.' Knowing how a proverb can encapsulate social beliefs helps to explain Hala's answers to my questions.

Zahra and Maisoon were the only two women who approved of divorce, although they were not taking any steps towards it:

> I just don't believe in divorce, although I badly wanted one. My husband used to be so irritable and attached to his mother. He even helped her financially, but after she died, no one needed his financial help any more. To tell you the truth, he isn't as irritable now as he used to be at the beginning of our marriage, so what could I possibly have told my parents? I can hardly have a reason for divorce in other people's opinion. (*Maisoon*)

This shows the dependence of Maisoon, like the majority of other women in Iraq, on other people's opinions.

Zahra told me this story:

> I want to divorce my husband but my family and his are preventing it. We started to have problems the first day we met. He raped me in the train on our wedding day when I was 13 years old. The problems got worse when we had our first baby.
>
> I was pregnant again two months after I had my first baby. I wanted to get divorced but this wouldn't have been legal because I was under age and my marriage wasn't legal anyway.[2] Each time I ran away my parents and relatives came and persuaded me to return. He promised my parents he would let me continue my studies and so he had to keep his promise, but he forced me to wear the *abaya* [black cloak] which even my mother didn't wear. I was successful in my studies and could have studied for an MA but he wouldn't allow it. However,

after many more problems and my running away to my parents, I managed to continue studying as I was living with my parents after having a big fight with him.

After much argument he allowed me to apply for a job, provided I handed over my salary to him every month, which I did. He then began to be awkward about giving me money for clothes and transport so I asked my parents to pay. The only expenses he didn't forbid were for food. He used to visit us every two months for ten days. During these ten days it was like being in hell. I suffered from depression and was admitted to hospital twice. I was taking medicine for a long time. I really tried to work for our marriage but it was impossible. He inflicted psychological and physical harm on me and I cannot forget it.

Suher's story, which follows, gave financial insecurity as a strong reason for rejecting divorce. Since her parents could not afford to have her back with her children, she continued to suffer. Her husband was jealous of her and accused her of having affairs and fathering both their children by another man. She told me:

Any talk which defames my dignity used to hurt me in the past, but now, insults have become a part of my life.

Her husband's mistreatment was due to lack of trust between them. He treated his children badly, thinking that they were not his own. In fact this accusation was unfounded; it merely reflects the suspicious mentality of some Iraqi men. Despite all this, Suher's attitude towards divorce was as follows:

Divorce has never occurred to me. I don't believe in it. I prefer desertion to divorce. I can't live alone. My husband is the one who thinks of divorce. He mentions it to me sometimes. I got fed up with him and asked him what he had done to me–referring to my responsibilities at home. Then he turned round and said if I didn't like it here I might as well leave home. He said, 'The door's wide enough for a camel to go through.' He once divorced me in the presence of his brother and my cousin. My cousin went and reported it to my mother, who came round to take me home with her. My daughter was eight months old; she needed milk and lots of other expenses. My family were not well off, so we went through some bad times. I returned to him six months later. After I had my second child, I was served with a court order for divorce. I was shocked. Yes, he always threatened me with divorce, but I didn't expect this, although I should have. He told me that he didn't think the baby was his, just because I discovered my pregnancy while he was abroad. Anyway, he didn't believe me when I told him, 'How could you? I'm a clean woman and there have been no other men in my life, not ever.' I just couldn't bear the idea of being a divorced woman, so I had to beg him to change his mind and I had to apologize for an offence I hadn't committed so as to stay with him. (*Suher*)

This indicates the extent to which a woman will put up with her husband's ill-treatment in order to keep her marriage going. Divorce is regarded as an impossibility. El Saadawi notes a similar case in Egypt. She explains how the law stands in such instances:

A husband may deny his fatherhood if a child is born earlier than six months after sexual intercourse with the woman or later than the maximum time limit for a full-term pregnancy (usually considered as one year) . . . the way of denying his parenthood of the child is by a procedure of repudiation called *la'an* (derived from *lan* which means 'curse'). This procedure consists in the father sending a complaint to the legal ruler . . . denying his fatherhood of the child, upon which the ruler will ask him to stand before him and testify to the fact. He must repeat four times, 'I testify before Allah that I am telling the truth when I maintain that this child is not of me [of my issue].' After having repeated these words . . . he is supposed to add, 'May I be cursed by Allah if I lied when I accused my wife and said that the child was not mine.' After the husband has borne witness, it is the turn of the wife. In conformity with the instructions of the ruler, she is supposed to say four times, 'I swear to Allah that my husband is lying when he accuses me of adultery.' Then, after having completed her testimony, she is supposed to say, 'May Allah's wrath smite me if my husband is telling the truth.' Judgement is then passed as a result of the *la'an*. Such a judgement may include denial of the man as parent of the child and perpetual separation between the man and the woman concerned.[3]

Many women mentioned children as a reason for not asking for divorce, but they forget that one parent could be better for a child than two with conflict between them. Financial considerations also come in here, and the thought that the children may suffer. Returning to the natal family is not always feasible:

Divorce is wrong, particularly if the couple has children. Would a woman be able to look after her children alone and bring them up without help? (*Ansam*)

I never think of divorce because of our children. Is it their fault? I wasn't wise to have children at the beginning of my marriage, but having no children is in fact an advantage in a divorce as the wife can easily go back to live with her parents again. (*Rafida*)

In retrospect, Rafida's comment is somewhat unrealistic. Although contraception is possible, it is not freely available, and in any case a woman would probably not think of divorce when planning a family!

Other reasons may make a woman think of divorce, but again the shame brought on the family will stop her actually divorcing:

> I first thought of divorce when I found out that he was going out with another woman. That woman came to see me once and I went mad. She just said she'd come to visit me. Imagine, she claimed that she was a relative of his!
>
> Finally I left home and stayed with my parents for four months. I also thought of divorce when my mother died. I was so depressed then and went to see many doctors. One day his family came to visit us and we had a problem between us which ended up with him beating me on my chest. I left home and suffered from a chest pain and a lump. A year later I was operated on as a result. However, I've been hesitant about divorce. Whenever I think of taking steps towards divorce, I regret them and change my mind. I think, why should I ruin my family? People have to be sensible and solve their problems patiently. (*Jamila*)

Despite all the problems outlined here, the main factor preventing frequent divorce remains the fact that a divorcee would find it difficult to remarry. The following quotation explains how women see divorce:

> Divorce itself creates problems. My sister is a divorcee, but she's very unhappy. She can't build another life for herself. (*Suha*)

Minai's work may help explain the background of these attitudes towards divorce although she describes a case from the eleventh century:

According to this fear-ridden attitude toward women, virginity was important in guaranteeing not only the legitimacy of heirs but also the bride's innocence; husbands feared being compared unfavourably to other men. Imam al-Ghazali, one of the most eminent theologians of the eleventh century, mentioned this point: 'The virgin will love her husband and get used to him, which will favourably influence marital relations . . . A woman who has had experience with other men or one who was married before will often compare her husband's peculiarities to those of other men and be dissatisfied.'[4]

In her 1956 research on Iraqi women, El-Bustani looked at the issue of independence for women. What is striking is the similarity between the answers of her interviewees and mine, despite the tremendous changes Iraq underwent in this period:

The consensus was that women are not equal to men; they are dominated by men and dependent upon men. 'No equal rights.' 'No equal treatment.' 'Men are more respected, more privileged and more preferred.' 'Women are dependent.' 'Women are less important.' These statements made by all the women interviewees imply that the existence of a double standard in Iraqi society pulls the two sexes apart.[5]

In conclusion, women's attitudes towards independence, both within and outside marriage, are linked with change in the whole social structure. Working women may feel stronger, as they have more money of their own and access to the support system that colleagues and friends may provide. Older women and more educated women who have responsible jobs may take the lead in this matter. When the women who are now working come to socialize their own children, they may wish not to bring them up in the way they were brought up, so the next generation may treat the freedom of women differently. This is speculation, however. In practice, women still treat their children very much as their mothers treated them.

Women's View of Liberation

Most women in Iraq have no knowledge of, or little comprehension of, the activities of the women's liberation movement and many disapprove of such developments. I asked if they had heard of the women's liberation movement, and if so, what their opinion of it was. Some said they had heard of it but they could not see any point in it, so far as their work was concerned, because:

> In our society, I think women are emancipated already. All these meetings–there's no need for them, they're just a waste of time. Our religion gives us all the rights we need. I also think these meetings and all this talk about women's rights make men resent women even more. Instead of all this, if every wife tried to understand her husband and every girl tried to understand her father and brothers, everybody would live in peace and there would be no need for all this fuss. (*Salwa*)

In connection with the ideology of honour and shame, the following answers were typical:

> I agree with women's liberation in so far as it doesn't lead to corruption. (*Haifa*)

Many women believed that women are already liberated in Iraq and need not push themselves any further in pursuit of equality. Others saw Iraqi women as successfully moving towards liberation, but all of them believed that the Western woman is not the ideal of the liberated woman, due to the sexual freedom she enjoys. The ideology of honour and shame which underlies these opinions makes it clear that this lies deep within the Iraqi woman's consciousness, where there is a conception that liberation is linked to corruption or dissolution through sexual activity. In Arabic the word for corruption sounds very like the word for freedom.[6]

Some women referred to this and stated that although they wanted freedom, they did not want it to extend to sexual corruption. Even though *tahalol* could describe other forms of corruption, the interviewees kept connecting the word with sexual corruption. The answers below are typical:

When defining the liberated woman I don't think of Western women. I want liberation for our women to be within the framework of our spiritual beliefs. Liberated women are not those who are interested in make-up and fashion. They're the ones who do their housework and duties in their jobs without degradation, the ones who take their chances in life and know their way, who have self-confidence. (*Nada*)

A conscious and an aware woman at home and in society is a liberated one. This is our concept of liberation. This differs from liberation in the West which is associated with corruption. (*Hala*)

A liberated woman is one who manages to earn people's respect. She should be free in going out and doing things, but know her 'limitations' and avoid dissolution. I don't know why, we always connect liberation with corruption.

Q: What are these 'limitations', and why in your opinion do we connect liberation with corruption?

A: There are some women who go as far as sitting on the bus in the middle of men and start smoking. Do you think that's nice? We should consider our society and traditions. It's true that men control us and they interfere even in our ways of dressing and our hair-styles but that doesn't mean we should liberate ourselves to the point of smoking in public. My husband believes that the GFIW[7] makes women disobedient, he doesn't agree at all with them, and to tell you the truth I agree with half of what he says. (*Suhad*)

If you take Western women's liberation, I don't believe in it, we hear a lot about the corruption there. (*Muna*)

If liberation means mixing with men, I disagree with it. I think the liberated woman is the educated woman who can use her education at home. (*Sawsan*)

Others believed that since women could now go to schools and colleges and hold jobs, that was enough. One woman believed that greater liberation for women would only cause problems and make women become masculine.

Several answers shed light on how women saw themselves as wives and mothers. Opinions ranged from those who believed a liberated woman was one who was 'happy' and 'successful' and who managed to combine her home commitments and her job, to one who was able to discuss things with her husband. There were some traditionalists who believed that women should be submissive, but the prevailing opinion was that women should avoid behaviour such as smoking in public or sitting with crossed legs, in short, any behaviour which might be thought 'low'. It is interesting that such behaviour was connected with women they thought liberated, and several women said that 'liberated' women smoked in public. Relatively more positive answers came from those who approved of education and work for those women who used their knowledge 'to make a happy home'.

From their answers, it seems reasonable to assume that all these women continued to be influenced by the ideology of honour and shame. The responses from all three categories of interviewees showed marked similarities and they all laid great emphasis on morality and honour in sexual matters. Without exception, they regarded European and American women as sexually permissive.

Most of the women I interviewed could not be called feminists. Although many of them were conscious of their oppression, they all saw this as an individual problem and their everyday behaviour merely encouraged such oppression. Perhaps their attitude towards their husband's helping with the housework was the most obvious example of this.

Conclusion

From the foregoing, it will be obvious that in Iraq women's oppression within the family is fairly universal. This chapter will compare Iraqi and Western women in the modern world in an attempt to reveal any change in the position of Iraqi women. Since it has been argued that paid work gives women independence, I shall examine what opportunities exist for education and paid work for women in Iraq and ask whether these opportunities have in fact proved beneficial. I shall also look at women within the household structure and discuss the nuclear family, which is becoming increasingly common with Westernization. Does this mean a better life for the modern Iraqi woman, away from the control of the in-laws, or is it even more restrictive?

Traditional Oppression and the Resulting Conflicts for Women

For many centuries women in Iraq have been controlled by men and a woman's life is planned for her in a complex manner almost from the moment of conception. Traditionally, women are socially isolated and confined to the home. They are considered to be weaker than men, both physically and mentally. A 'good woman' is one who is obedient and submissive. She is taught to serve others and to treat her parents, older brothers, senior members of the family, her husband and his family with respect. Her mother is her ideal. A girl should be the guardian of the family honour by being virginal and pure. After marriage, however, she should keep her chaste outlook and not develop any interest in being independent.

Most women in Iraq still know nothing more about their future husband than his name and appearance, some information about his family and financial status, and particularly his level of education. They know almost nothing about his personality; therefore, according to many of those I interviewed and the majority of Iraqi women, marriage is based more on what is considered to be fate and luck than on real feelings and an intimate relationship; it is a plan based on materialistic factors, which often causes difficulties later on in life. Most of the women I spoke to had thought that they would develop a relationship based on love and understanding with their husband after marriage, as the years passed. When they did not manage to do so, they began to blame themselves for this failure, although regarding it as their fate, which must be accepted. This explains their response to the cultural theme of passive acceptance of fate. All the women expressed in one way or the other their acceptance of *qisma wa nasseeb*, that is, fate and destiny. This is a deeply held belief, particularly in rural Iraq, which is frequently applied to marriage.

It must be remembered that the family was, and still is, very strong in the Arab world; the changing family structure (from extended to nuclear) has hardly loosened family ties.

From the answers to my questions, it is clear that Iraqi women are oppressed in society as a whole; marriage as an institution is controlled by men and based on power rather than equality, which results in the subordination of women to men within the family.

Despite the fact that girls see many unhappy marriages around them, they still feel very strongly that marriage is their most important aim in life. This is primarily due to the socialization process, which teaches that marriage is the major event in a girl's life: it is her reward for playing her role well. If a woman behaves in accordance with social expectations, she will be regarded as honourable; if not, she will be regarded as dishonourable and punished by gossip, which affects her reputation and therefore her chances of marriage.

Divorcees, widows and spinsters, although occupying different positions in society, all occupy a lower position than married women. This reinforces the importance of marriage and gives girls stronger motives to seek marriage, and even to keep up an unhappy marriage. Widows have a relatively better status than divorcees and spinsters, however, as it is believed to be God's will for their husband to die, while a divorced woman is herself assumed to be the reason for her divorce. As for a spinster, it is assumed that she has some flaw which has prevented her from marrying. This explains why many spinsters mention the number of men who asked for their hand in marriage, and say that either their families or they themselves refused in the hope of a better match (which never occurred).

Most of the women I interviewed were in a nuclear family, in line with the trend in today's Iraq. Those who had lived with their in-laws at the beginning of their marriage did so for financial rather than traditional reasons and as soon as they managed to get their own house they moved out. Siham was living with her mother rather than her in-laws: her husband was doing his military service, so she needed help with the children and was afraid to live on her own. Wafaa's mother-in-law was living with her because she was an old woman and needed her son and his family to look after her. Only two women (Bahira and Nazhat, both housewives) lived in the traditional setting of an extended family. Even in these two cases, both women indicated that in a few years' time, if their husbands managed to build houses for them, they would move out.

It should be noted that older people traditionally enjoy more power than younger ones within the family. This kind of power, which is acquired with age, applies to every sector of traditional society. When women get older and daughters-in-law start coming into the household, the mother-in-law (as a senior woman) controls the younger women and becomes a powerful figure within the household. With the growth of the nuclear family in the modern urban sector, the situation is changing and older women cannot exercise the same power as they did in the past. They might live with their daughters or sons but not as heads of the household.

Nevertheless, older women still enjoy better status. It is important here to distinguish between status and power. Although old people might lose the power they used to exercise, they do not lose the status they enjoy through trust and respect, whether within the family or the whole of society. Elderly people are not only respected and trusted by their families, but also served by them; the younger generation try to meet their every need. In comparing older women in traditional families as heads of households with older women nowadays, the latter are respected but no longer make the important decisions such as whether the family should buy a car, move house, and so on.

All older women are expected to be sexually inactive. In a society where male honour is connected with and dependent upon female sexual behaviour within the family, the issue becomes especially important: as women get older they can be trusted more by men in the family, and they start policing younger women to meet the same expectations of trust. In the traditional family, younger women show older women respect mixed with fear, but not admiration–older women are pitied because of their age and because they can no longer produce children.

When sexually active, women are constantly controlled and watched until they reach what is called *sin al-yaas*, the age of no hope. This social belief affects every aspect of women's lives at this age, as some women enter the menopause at 40. Starting from this age, and particularly if a woman is widowed, she will wear dark coloured clothes, in most cases black, for the rest of her life. She will wear very little or no make-up and restrict her activities, in order to be *imraa wa koora, wa razina*, 'a respectable woman'.[1]

When talking about a sexually active age for women, I am not referring to how women see themselves or to their actual sex life but to the age at which men are interested in them. (As sex is one area in particular where women feel reserved and prudish, even within marriage, most of the women I interviewed took no initiative in it.) However, women might gain a relatively better status and some power within the family from this age, as they will not attract the attention of other men and so will be trusted by their own male family members. Women gain similar status when having children, and for the same reason: men's interest in them will be much less than in those women who do not have children. In other words, women's ties to their children will strengthen their ties with their husband and other men will be less attracted to them.

The Iraqi woman's life is a series of conflicts. There is the conflict between, on the one hand, the desire to be independent and have a career and, on the other hand, the wish to appear dependent and weak to fit the stereotype of 'feminine behaviour'. For example, in Chapter 7 several women said they wished they had been born men, because men enjoy more freedom than women. A woman, however, must not act in the least like a man in order not to be termed masculine and lose the chance of finding a husband. Similarly, girls are sometimes prevented from taking a higher degree or demanding a better job in the belief that this might stop them getting married. Paradoxically, while women are prepared for marriage from a very early age and carefully brought up to see it as their main objective, they are at the same time expected not to talk about marriage or even think about it.

Firestone has said that 'Love is used by men to control women in the West'.[2] The opposite is true in Iraq. Women do not express love for men before marriage, as it is shameful; therefore 'not to show love' is the man's method of control. In short, Iraqi society turns the Western notion of love on its head. In Iraq, a wife's love for her husband is encouraged only in the form of serving and obeying him, rather than in words of affection and loving behaviour. Such Western attitudes are not yet acceptable in Iraqi society although very much admired by Iraqi women.

Universal Oppression

The universal phenomenon of the oppression of women has taken different forms and been related to different ideologies and beliefs. Mernissi explains that while sexual inequality in Western culture is based on 'a belief in women's biological inferiority, there is no parallel belief in Islam'. Quite the reverse is true: the Islamic system 'is based on the assumption that the woman is a powerful and dangerous sexual being'.[3] Sharma, however, has observed similar attitudes in non-Muslim communities in India, where there is a widespread belief that female sexuality is more difficult to control than that of men.[4]

If women's sexuality is indeed 'dangerous' and more 'difficult to control than that of men' this implies that it is real. On the other hand, as revealed by the responses of my interviewees, men's attitude denies the existence of female sexuality. These two contradictory social beliefs are both used to control women. The very fact that most Iraqi women manage to get married implies that they are honourable and that, unlike prostitutes, they are not interested in sex. However, all the forms of social control practised over women suggest that they are 'dangerous sexual beings' and must be controlled. When most of the women I interviewed derived no sexual satisfaction from their marriage and some of them did not know what an orgasm was, how can their sexuality be considered 'dangerous'?[5]

As shown in Chapter 1 with reference to honour and shame and their connection with sexual behaviour, and in the women's answers to my questions on this point, extra-marital sex is usually only for men. Furthermore, sexual relations–whether before marriage or in an extra-marital relationship–are seen as 'liberal' and 'modern' when practised by men. Within the family, the father appears to be more liberal and open-minded about sexual practices. Women rather than men are the guardians of male domination, by controlling children and restricting them to specific rules and forms of behaviour.

Options for Change

The husband/wife relationship appeared unsatisfactory to all the women I questioned, particularly the housewives and teachers, although most saw their problems in individual terms and related them to their fate. Nevertheless, all of them had complaints and grievances. They pointed especially to the lack of understanding between themselves and their husbands. Most found it difficult to find a common topic of conversation with their husband apart from talking about the children. Sex was a taboo subject and was never mentioned to them by other adults in their families before marriage. None of the women had any reliable information about it and the concept of virginity appeared to be a source of anxiety and fear. Most said they were scared and shocked when they menstruated for the first time. Sex was regarded as a hated duty.

Recent developments and modernization in Iraqi society, with all the social mobility, provision of education, employment and communication through the media, was meant to improve women's lives, among other aims. However, their ideas and practices are still backward when compared to those of men. The tradition of patriarchy is almost untouched by these changes, all of which results in further conflict for women, as will be seen later on in this chapter.

The school curriculum in Iraq includes pictures, texts and ideas which support the traditional role of women as mainly wives and mothers, and men as breadwinners and heads of the household. Iraqi films, plays and songs also enforce the ideology of male domination. It is still a man's world and educational programmes and school curricula have not taken any steps to give women the very basic knowledge which would enable them to make small household repairs or to handle kitchen equipment.

Traditional values imply that women exist only to serve men and produce children. If they have any ability at all, if they are intelligent or well-educated, it is implied that they should use these abilities to improve their home, so as to please men and to bring up children in an appropriate manner. This ideology suggests that most of the problems children suffer from, and most of the unhappy homes and dissatisfied husbands, are all related to women who neglect their homes and pay too much attention to their work. These are the kind of ideas and beliefs often represented in the Iraqi media. From my data it is apparent that a large number of women also subscribe to these ideas.

Another important factor in women's current situation in Iraq is legislation and the way in which the law is applied. Women have customarily felt that it is not honourable for them to go to court. Consequently, they lose all their legal rights. In those cases where a woman decides to ask for her rights, despite social dislike of such behaviour, she receives no support of any kind from her parents or family. This effectively puts a stop to all legal action because women are unable to disobey the family upon whom they depend.[6]

In addition, legislation on the personal status of women still lags behind that for men. For example, men who commit 'honour crimes' (in which a woman is killed for real or supposed adultery) often go unpunished. Another example is the legal attitude towards extra-marital sexual relations, for which severe and absolute punishments are inflicted on women, while only mild punishments are applied to men.

Another problem, rarely acknowledged by women, is their lack of participation in decision-making at government level. The number of women in high posts is insufficient to influence decision-making; this is surprising in a system which encourages women's participation in every sphere of government employment. The low numbers are perhaps attributable to the attitudes of the administrative system, which is still strongly affected by traditional beliefs. An even stronger reason is, as discussed earlier, the lack of ambition in women themselves. Women may avoid holding high posts in the belief that it may reduce their chances of marriage or (if they are already married) have a harmful effect on their marital relationship.

Another reason behind the lack of women's participation in decision-making is that not all women in high positions are necessarily concerned to improve women's lives in society and within the family, even by providing them with services and machinery to help them with the housework. Some of the women who are able to influence decision-making seem to be political ostriches in this respect. The few who believe in women's liberation and manage to reach influential positions face an uphill struggle.

As mentioned previously, the system of male domination in Iraqi society uses Islamic ideology and bedouin social values as tools to control women, despite the fact that these two ideologies are distinct and, at some points, opposed to each other. Similarly, other cultures and ideas with which Iraqis have come into contact have been used to oppress women, while the positive aspects of such cultures have had little impact. Western culture has influenced Iraqi men and women in different ways, which results in some women's impatience with 'modernity'. According to al-Hibri,[7] the Western view of women as inherently inferior has combined with the traditional view that women must be controlled, with the result that women have 'progressed' to the worst of both worlds, as shown elsewhere in this book.

The Impact of Modernization

The way in which women's lives are developing in contemporary Iraq shows that they are losing many of the positive aspects of traditional life, while they are moving towards the adoption of some Western ways of living. They seem to be adopting the negative aspects of Westernization, especially having to do two jobs without a change in attitudes towards housework. They allow men to use them even more by adopting the contemporary desire to be fashionable at all costs. Many women in Iraq care for fashion almost as much as models do in the West; it controls their minds, time and money. The nuclear family isolates women from relatives and deprives them of their help. (Research has shown that this results in isolation for women in capitalist societies.[8]) This comes without any change in child-rearing practices or ways of cooking, or any increased independence like that of Western women, as well a gradual loss of solidarity with their own sex. As they move closer to adopting Western ways of living, Iraqi women are losing rather than improving their quality of life. Everyday activities for Western women such as sport, membership of clubs, and so on, are far from being adopted by Iraqi women.

This loss allows further male domination. As Beck and Keddie[9] observe, 'female association, powerful in cultures where social institutions and values inhibit most efforts by women to establish solidarity with one another, can challenge male domination'.

While female associations in Arab culture have always been encouraged, modernization discourages such solidarity and it is not observed among modern Iraqi women in any form.

Perhaps the major difference between a modern urban Iraqi woman and her Western counterpart is the way the former perceives herself in terms of her relationship with her natal family and in no way as an individual being. Consequently the idea of independence which Western women live and practise, which is accepted by them and society, does not exist in Iraq. For example, if an Iraqi working woman decides to support herself and leaves her husband, or if she is not married and decides to live alone, away from her natal family (a situation which is very common amongst Western women), she must prepare herself to fight: everyone will be against her, her reputation might be tarnished and she will lose the support of relatives, friends and everyone she cares for. In short, she will be isolated socially and this might even affect her job.[10]

The women I spoke to frequently stressed the cultural importance of relating individually to their families as their means of self-evaluation. Whenever they had a quarrel with their husband, they told him:

You're talking to so-and-so's daughter, you seem to have forgotten that. (*Muna*)

You didn't pick me up from the streets. What if my brothers knew how you were treating me? (*Jamila*)

From such statements, it is clear that women assess themselves on the basis of family status and the family name, which is not often the case with Western women. When a Western woman separates from her husband, whether through death or divorce, this affects her very differently from her Arab counterpart, both emotionally and financially. For an Arab woman, the consequences are far more severe because they affect the roots of her very identity. To start with, losing a husband means being dependent on the natal family again, even in the case of a working woman, because she is not permitted to live alone. It also means that she constantly has to defend herself against a social crime she has not committed, but is expected to commit at any time because she is no longer a virgin–that is, engaging in a sexual relationship. It is as if virginity were the guardian of women rather than their own consciousness. In short, a divorced woman enjoys much lower status than a married one. Women feel that losing a husband might cost them everything in life. This explains the low divorce rate in Iraq. In the West, on the other hand, it is common for women to live away from their natal family, from as early as 18 years of age, and whether they have a husband or not. Western women do not then need to depend on their natal family again. Iraqi women feel that they belong to their natal family and have much stronger ties with it than with their husband. This might also explain why women tend not to develop any emotional feelings towards their husband; they see him as an outsider who might leave them at any time, whereas the natal family will never do so. As noted in Chapter 4, this creates 'bad feelings' between the husband and his in-laws.

Has Education Made any Difference?

Education for girls has grown rapidly in Iraqi society and this applies particularly to higher education. Most of the interviewees' mothers were illiterate. It is Iraqi government policy for education and all kinds of jobs to be open to women. Primary school education is compulsory, as are illiteracy eradication classes. In urban areas, the percentage of girls attending high school is almost the same as that of boys. In higher education the majority of the students are girls, particularly in the humanities.

Nevertheless a major problem remains: that of male disapproval of the changes directed towards improving women's position. Education for girls is still regarded primarily as an additional qualification for marriage and a way of gaining increased status.[11] This may have been a factor in encouraging the education of girls in contemporary Iraq.

Despite the high percentage of educated urban women in Iraq, society still expects a woman to refuse to marry a man who is less educated than herself. (The definition of 'educated' in this sense only means qualifications, diplomas, and so on, not real knowledge.) If such an 'unequal' marriage took place, it would create great anxiety for the wife–most women try hard to pretend in everyday life that they are not as knowledgeable as their husbands. Such a belief helps to prevent women from gaining higher education. The choice is between finding a husband, and getting another degree and losing the chance of marriage.

Minai suggests a number of reasons why girls are handicapped within the educational system; the harem mentality exerts an important influence over women, who are still bound by the code of honour. Education has inevitably brought Muslim women into conflict with traditional culture. Although education has broadened women's horizons, they are still subject to restrictions at home which guard their reputation (and hence their family's reputation) with a view to enhancing their marriageability.[12] This is not to imply that no changes have occurred in women's lives, but they have not lived up to expectations, nor have they kept pace with other changes in society.

Let us briefly look at some of positive changes which have accompanied women's improved access to education. One important factor is the reduction in the number of children; there is a clear correlation between level of education and smaller family size. The other factor is the veil, or what anthropologists call purdah, which is ending rapidly, particularly among educated women. Only one of the women I interviewed (a teacher) had worn the veil. I would argue that the number of unveiled women has increased due to women's education, rather than to that of men.[13] One result has been that couples are starting to go out together. This new phenomenon has created great anxiety for women. Education has also affected the system of arranged marriage in the sense that couples are allowed to see each other first, but to choose a man for life after only a few chaperoned meetings is obviously unsatisfactory for an educated woman.

All my research shows that the contemporary, educated urban Iraqi woman is dissatisfied with her social position. This dissatisfaction results from a growing awareness brought about by social change. The older generation were satisfied because they were less well informed; they accepted their subordination, seeing it as a 'good deed' for women. The main difference between the two generations is that the contemporary woman experiences a greater degree of ambiguity in her life, including the fundamental aspects of family life, her relationship with men and her place at work. Although social change has resulted in raising women's consciousness to some extent, when it is not accompanied by changes in men's attitudes it is merely a disadvantage for women.

When discussing the changing roles of men and women, and observing the strength of traditional beliefs and values in connection with society's expectations of women, Nelson states (in relation to Egypt) that there has been a shift in the concept of the ideal woman–away from the submissive, passive, ignorant one to an independent partner for the man. But whether men recognize this ideal is another matter.[14] A similar comment could be made about Iraqi society.

Both men and women in Iraq tend to perceive tasks within the home as being a natural obligation for women. Most women blame themselves for conflicts or breakdowns in their marital relationship. They generally see their problems as being theirs alone rather than perceiving them as part of a wider, deeply embedded social practice between the sexes. Such individualization of problems inhibits any kind of collective political action for women.

The other major difference between the two generations (which applies more to educated women than to illiterate housewives) is a change in the husband's violence from physical to mental. Several women, from all three categories, stated that their father used to beat their mother and shouted at them and the children. Many of the housewives said that their husband beat them and all of them had husbands who were irritable and frequently shouted at them. While most of the educated women complained about their irritable husband, almost all revealed clearly that his violence against them was mental rather than physical:

> He never allows me to express my opinion when we're with others; he always shuts me up and disagrees with anything I say. He always makes fun of me. (*Muna*)

> He compares me with other women who he thinks are much better than me in every way. (*Zahida*)

Has Paid Work Made any Difference?
In rural Arab society, women do most of the work in the fields and receive little or no money in return. This means that they are a vital asset to the productive system and one would expect a female child to be a welcome addition to the workforce. Yet in a traditional rural setting, the birth of a son is a much happier occasion than the birth of a girl. Women are often divorced by their husband because they bear them no sons.

Although men and women in Iraq receive similar pay for work of equal value, the idea that women should be supported by men is still widespread in society. Owing to their socialization, the majority of urban Arab women seem to feel that work is a natural role for them after completing their education, but paid work is regarded as a secondary activity for women. Thus work has only a limited influence on their independence. Iraqi women appear to enter the labour market automatically after leaving school or college and are unlikely to leave their job after marriage or even after the arrival of their first baby.

In her research on Indian women, Sharma found that for women, their outside work is subordinate to their role as wives rather than to their role as mothers.[15] This is very similar to my findings on Iraqi women. It may also explain why Iraqi women continue to work after the arrival of their babies since they too see their role as a wife as more important. (Their husband also usually demands extra help with their financial situation.)

The working women I interviewed had all been brought up to see themselves as working women. But in some cases their family had interfered in their choice of studies, not allowing their daughter to go for a challenging job which could bring her independence. Nevertheless all the women wanted their daughters to study any subject of their choice and to have a good job after completing their education. This applied not only to educated working women but also to housewives. Only two women felt that a girl's destiny might demand otherwise, and that finding the right man came before education and a job. In these cases, the families did not want education to stand in the way of their daughters' marriage but if the husband did not mind, their daughters could continue their studies. Such attitudes never-theless reveal an awareness that the social values that applied to the mothers were no longer valid for the daughters.

As for the women's attitudes towards their own job, the

majority did not see their work as a way of acquiring status. Most made it plain that they were not interested in their job and wanted to leave if they could afford to do so. However, in the majority of cases it was housework rather than financial reasons which kept the women working. The following is a typical answer:

> I'd give up, I'm not very interested in my work, but I'm afraid that I might get fed up at home. (*Siham*)

This might indicate that paid work increases women's independence, which contradicts my earlier argument. It is true that women do obtain a little more power through work outside the home, but the limitation of this power and its extremely slow increase (in comparison with men's power, for example), particularly for women within the family, shows the paralysing effect of their own socialization.

When the job itself is not very interesting, life becomes even harder, which leads women to say:

> Yes, I'd give up my job and devote myself to looking after my home and my children. I'm content, unlike other women. I don't mind staying at home. I might be relaxed and it would be better than my situation at home now, you know. (*Feryal*)

It is clear that there has not been much improvement in the situation of working women in Iraq. Although work offers some form of increased social status, the losses involved in working equalize the situation, particularly if we bear in mind that women's position within the family does not offer much change in their status. A job nevertheless represents financial security for women, to a limited extent within marriage and to a greater extent when the marriage ends. It should be noted that Iraqi society sees all manual jobs as degrading. For example, a worker in a beauty salon (who earns at least 80 Iraqi dinars a week) has a much lower status than a clerk in an office (who perhaps earns only 20 Iraqi dinars), although their educational qualifications may be similar.

The highest percentage of women workers is in teaching (in mixed schools, girls' schools and boys' schools), which is considered to be the most respectable and honourable job for women. Many women also have clerical jobs in mixed offices. It is worth noting that women in the Arab world, and in the Middle East in general, have gained a footing in the top professions, whereas women in the West have traditionally been restricted to low-status jobs. Girls in the West who are attracted to medicine but do not wish to study for gruelling medical exams might take up nursing. But in the Arab world nursing is considered to be a menial and low-grade job, and a girl who could not become a doctor would not become a nurse. From Turkey to Saudi Arabia, women seek jobs in the top professions, mainly teaching, medicine and law.[16] If a woman's profession carries high status, it is then considered honourable, despite the fact that it might put her in direct contact with men.

In jobs which require minimal qualifications, the percentage of working women is very low. Iraqi women seek office, clerical and professional jobs which demand qualifications, so it has become essential for a girl to have a degree.

One of the major remaining handicaps is that of social attitudes towards women in high positions. Simone de Beauvoir's comment remains true today: women eagerly seek out professional men, but neither men nor women like to work for a woman.[17] I tested women's attitudes toward professional women and those in high positions by asking the question, 'Would you rather work for a man or a woman boss or manager, and why?' Only four of the working women replied that they simply wanted to work for a competent, educated boss or manager, regardless of sex. Two other women said they would prefer a woman boss as they would not feel comfortable working with a man (again this does not mean they would prefer to work for a woman if she were competent; rather, this implies traditionalist reservations). The large majority of women indicated in one way or another that they would prefer male bosses:

Women are emotional and unsure of themselves . . . men are more capable.(*Suha*)

Men do not follow routine procedure as women do. Life is much easier under male managers. (*Rafida*)

Men are more broad-minded. Their approach is more relaxed and flexible. They do not fear their shadows, as women do. (*Lufia*)

Men are sympathetic and polite, whereas women want only to find faults in other women in order to be used against them. They envy each other. (*Suhad*)

Men are more advanced in their way of thinking . . . Women bosses are tough and hard, trying to prove themselves. (*Sabiha*)

When I asked whether they would prefer to work only with women rather than in a mixed office, those who said yes explained that they preferred to work freely in an atmosphere where they did not need to be careful how they sat or laughed, for example (as they would have to do if they worked with men). The majority saw many disadvantages in working with women only, as women tended to be jealous and to talk about each other behind their backs. The following answer is typical:

Women are silly. They talk about marriage, housework, children, etc. But if you work in an environment with men, they talk about philosophy, politics, art. I like these types of discussion. At least you learn something. (*Hala*)[18]

If, as Hunt suggests, ideology is a body of beliefs which are accepted without question and traditions can be considered as ideologies, then traditions are inherently conservative. Thus it is not surprising that women's progress in the field of work has had little effect on their traditional status in the family.[19]

In her research on working women in Iraq, Qasim discovered that one of the most important factors encouraging women to work is financial, as their wages improve their family's standard of living. Nevertheless, 77% of the working women in her sample showed deep conflicts with their family as a result of working. 82% of the mothers who left their children at nurseries or kindergartens were not satisfied, saying that they could not look after children the way mothers do. Qasim also found that 87% of the mothers showed a high degree of conflict and had difficulty in managing their work as well as doing all the housework and child-caring, bearing in mind that their husband's participation in either was very limited. Women in general were not interested in their job. Work was often 'routine' for them, the reason being that the jobs do not live up to the women's expectations.[20] I found very similar attitudes among women I interviewed.

In today's urban situation, where women are working outside the home as well as being forced to provide domestic labour, the loss of the general support system (material and emotional) associated with the extended family means that conditions for educated working women have become much worse. The combined responsibility for domestic work and child-care weakens women's power position both at home and at work, with the trend towards the nuclear family. This is leading to the same problems for working women in Iraq as in Europe. Women have become free to take paid professional work but this has not allowed them to abrogate their responsibilities to husbands and children.[21]

Domestic Work and Paid Work: the Undervaluation of Women's Labour

One of the most important problems facing working women today is how to combine housework and child-care. The culturally embedded belief that housework and looking after children is 'women's work' is a universal problem for women. Nevertheless such problems have been eased in the modern Western world by a relatively more positive male attitude and conveniences such as pre-cooked food, child-care facilities, and so on.

In Iraq women are still socialized to believe that men are superior to them. They do not allow their husband to help with the housework as it is considered an inferior job. Husbands only do minor tasks such as preparing the salad, although women (especially those with a job outside the home) need their husband's help. The women themselves perpetuate the traditional division of labour. They experience a conflict between their desire to be a 'proper' wife and their wish for free time to enjoy visiting friends and relatives.

Many Iraqi working women, due to the dual burden of job and housework, find it difficult to go out and socialize with friends. Sometimes they find it hard to see even their own families and relatives. This is a particularly important issue in women's lives. Men, however, go out with friends almost every evening.

As for the housewives, men see themselves as the providers: they keep their wives. In return, wives should perform the services at home. Where the wives are working women, however, they are not 'kept' as housewives–they perform domestic work for nothing.[22]

As research from many different societies has shown, house-work has never been valued in economic terms. This leaves women with no sense of value as a group and ignores the fact that men's labour would be paralysed if it were not for the unpaid labour of women at home. The nature of the services women provide deprives them of power and of material resources. This partly explains why Iraqi women wish to find a rich husband, so that they can have help with the housework.

In theory, one of the important aims of the women's movement in Iraq is to raise women's consciousness: to change their way of thinking, to help them to be more positive, to narrow the gap between women and men within society, and to recognize the attitudes towards women and their subsequent inferiority. It is clear from my interviews that this has not yet been achieved. 'Liberation' is seen as a private matter, not one which is susceptible to political action. Liberation affects the honour of the individual woman, and as she is brought up to believe that she is the guardian of her own and her family's honour, she must not be too liberated, particularly if she is to fit into the category of a 'good woman'.

Urban women in Iraq have been exposed to Westernization and modernization while rural woman have not. The majority of urban women now receive an education and a large percentage participate in the workforce. Although their consciousness has been raised, this has merely led to added anxiety and complexity in their lives. While working-class women and rural women might suffer from physical violence, educated women in the cities face more extreme types of mental violence from their husbands and other men in the family. The situation is not appreciated by Western feminists who argue that women in the middle and upper classes do not suffer from oppression as working class and rural women do.

The answers to my questions showed that most of the women

experienced a sense of inferiority within the family. Some of them talked about it, while others tried not to. A telling fact was that forty of the fifty interviewees expressed their regret at getting married.

In general, despite the fact that most educated women see their sex as occupying an inferior position in society, they tend to see their experience within the family in individual terms rather than as a general phenomenon. Most of the women in all three categories felt that it was their bad luck which led them to marry a particular man. Few of them mentioned other men who asked for their hand in marriage.

The individualization of problems has bolstered the patriarchal system's oppression of women, particularly within the institution of marriage and in preventing them from organizing to end this oppression. As already indicated, the embedded concept of femininity is based on a calculated socialization process which prevents recent legislation from having any substantive effect. The family is the major factor in shaping women and it continues to operate within both traditional and modern systems. The strong family ties help to maintain the system of patriarchy, because in the family individual women are socialized for a sexually differentiated role, which perpetuates their subordinate status. In brief, neither legislation nor educational policies have made any real impact on the oppression of Iraqi women.

From my research, it appears that Iraqi women in general were speaking out against themselves and against their freedom. On the whole, they looked down on women and did not approve of working under them. It is therefore clear that socialization has been very successful in reinforcing the patriarchal system. In conclusion, the recent modernization of Iraqi society in terms of social and economic changes has had a negative impact on women. Their role has merely become more complicated and their lifestyle more stressful and anxiety-provoking.

Appendix I: Personal Information about Interviewees and their Families

Woman interviewed	Age at time of interviews	Age at marriage		No. of siblings (incl. self)	No. of children
		Wife	Husband		
HOUSEWIVES					
Amal	33	20	30	7	4
Amina	26	18	26	7	2
Bahira	23	15	24	6	2
Fawzia	42	13	29	12	7
Gamila	35	17	35	11	7
Iqbal	32	25	35	4	3
Jamila	30	12	25	8	0
Khadija	38	13	28	5	3
Labiba	37	20	30	8	5
Majida	37	15	26	8	6
Nabiha	39	12	30	11	1
Nadira	38	14	29	12	5
Nazhat	20	19	30	8	1
Rahima	18	15	35	9	2
Sahira	28	15	32	9	5
Zahida	34	29	30	3	3
TEACHERS					
Ansam	35	23	34	9	0
Fatima	22	21	35	8	Pregnant
Feryal	40	22	30	10	4
Haifa	42	21	32	4	3
Ibtihal	32	22	32	10	3
Jumana	50	29	32	7	6
Maisoon	36	18	38	6	2
Muna	36	19	34	11	4
Nazira	45	28	40	7	4
Rafida	33	23	33	12	2
Sabiha	28	24	34	4	3
Salwa	40	29	40	5	0
Samar	40	18	29	4	4
Sawsan	40	23	35	3	0
Shada	20	18	24	11	1

Woman interviewed	Age at time of interviews	Age at marriage		No. of siblings (incl. self)	No. of children
		Wife	*Husband*		
Siham	35	19	28	6	2
Suha	30	25	30	5	2
Suhad	34	30	35	4	2
Wafaa	36	25	35	7	3
Zainab	35	29	32	7	3
HIGHER PROFESSIONALS					
Ahlam	48	22	23	5	4
Baidaa	36	31	35	7	1
Fadwa	53	28	35	8	0
Fatin	42	23	24	8	3
Hajir	37	35	40	10	1
Hala	42	29	35	8	2
Huda	38	25	33	7	2
Lutfia	36	20	27	2	2
Madiha	32	22	30	10	3
Nada	57	38	42	2	1
Najwa	55	22	30	7	5
Suher	30	17	29	10	2
Sumia	38	23	24	3	1
Zahra	30	13	33	7	2

Appendix II: Education, Qualifications and Occupations of Interviewees and their Families

Woman interviewed	Husband's occupation	Father's occupation	Woman's education	Husband's education	Father's education
HOUSEWIVES					
Amal	Printer	Lorry driver	2nd yr IEC	Primary	None
Amina	Accountant	Shopkeeper	3rd yr IEC	BA	Some
Bahira	Assistant director	Colonel	3rd yr IEC	BA	High school
Fawzia	Café owner	Bus driver	3rd yr IEC	Some	Some
Gamila	Butcher	Butcher	Some IEC	Some	Some
Iqbal	Tailor	Unemployed	2nd yr IEC	High school	Primary
Jamila	Bookseller	Lorry driver	3rd yr IEC	High school	Some
Khadija	Clerk	Printer	2nd yr IEC	High school	None
Labiba	Lorry driver	Dustman	Some IEC	Some	None
Majida	Technician	Baker	2nd yr IEC	Primary	Some
Nabiha	Taxi driver	Mosque employee	Some IEC	High school	None
Nadira	Clerk	Postman	Some IEC	High school	None
Nazhat	Clerk	Usher	3rd yr IEC	BA	Primary
Rahima	Electrician	Conductor	1st yr IEC	Primary	Primary
Sahira	Teacher	Merchant	2nd yr IEC	BA	Some
Zahida	Accountant	Goldsmith	3rd yr IEC	BA	Primary
TEACHERS					
Ansam	Clerk	Typist	Diploma	BA	Primary
Fatima	Chemist	Colonel	Diploma	BSc	High school
Feryal	Dir. of Min. of Education	Chief clerk	Diploma	BSc	High school
Haifa	High school teacher	Librarian	BA	BA	High school
Ibtihal	Chemist	Shopkeeper	BA	BSc	High school
Jumana	Assistant director	Journalist	BA	BSc	High school
Maisoon	Hospital director	Administrator	BA	FRCS	High school
Muna	Primary school teacher	Car dealer	Diploma	Diploma	Some

Woman interviewed	Husband's occupation	Father's occupation	Woman's education	Husband's education	Father's education
Nazira	Colonel	Estate owner	BA	BA	High school
Rafida	High school teacher	Mechanic	BSc	BSc	Primary
Sabiha	Lieutenant	Teacher	Diploma	BA	High school
Salwa	Military attaché	Town clerk	Diploma	MA	High school
Samar	Architect	Clerk	Diploma	MSc	Primary
Sawsan	Major-general	Clerk	BA	MSc	High school
Shada	Sergeant	Tailor	Diploma	High school	Some
Siham	Major-general	Accountant	BA	BA	High school
Suha	College teacher	Shopkeeper	Diploma	BA	Primary
Suhad	Laboratory assistant	Major	BSc	BA	High school
Wafaa	Colonel	Chief constable	BA	BSc	High school
Zainab	Lieutenant	Lieutenant	BA	BA	High school
HIGHER PROFESSIONALS					
Ahlam	Diplomat	Colonel	MA	MA	High school
Baidaa	Restaurant manager	Ex-minister	MA	BA	BA
Fadwa	Engineer	School inspector	BA	BSc	High school
Fatin	Chemist	Dep. chief constable	BSc	BSc	High school
Hajir	Under-minister	Clerk	MA	BSc	High school
Hala	Colonel	Oil co. worker	BA	BA	Some
Huda	University lecturer	Teacher	BA	PhD	High school
Lutfia	Cultural attaché	Librarian	BA	BA	High school
Madiha	Engineer	Journalist	BA	BA	High school
Nada	Company director	Teacher	MA	MA	High school

Woman interviewed	Husband's occupation	Father's occupation	Woman's education	Husband's education	Father's education
Najwa	Club director	Judge	High school	BA	High school
Suher	Geologist	Postman	High school	MSc	Some
Sumia	Head of dept. at ministry	Lawyer	BA	BA	High school
Zahra	Colonel	Businessman	BA	BA	High school

IEC = Illiteracy eradication centre.

Notes

1. Diploma = a certificate from a Teacher Training Centre. One year's study qualifies a student as a primary school teacher. High school graduates are accepted on this diploma course.

2. In the 'education' categories, 'some' indicates that a person is in the first year at an illiteracy eradication centre and can hardly read and write. Many students had to repeat a year.

3. Of the mothers of the 50 women interviewed, 4 were primary school teachers and 46 were housewives. Three had a high school education, 2 had attended primary school and 45 were illiterate.

Notes

Introduction

1. Ali al-Wardi, *A Study of Iraqi Society* (Irshad Press, Baghdad, 1965. In Arabic).

2. Ali al-Wardi, *Social Aspects of Modern Iraqi History*, part 1 (Irshad Press, Baghdad, 1969. In Arabic), p.298. See also R. Patai, *The Arab Mind* (Scribner's, New York, 1973), p.93.

3. Morroe Berger, *The Arab World Today* (Doubleday, New York, 1964).

4. Illiteracy eradication centres were set up all over Iraq in accordance with the 1978 law for the eradication of illiteracy. Attendance is compulsory for all those between the ages of 15 and 45 who are illiterate.

5. At the time of the interviews (1982) this meant salaries in the region of 80 Iraqi dinars (approx. £160) per month.

6. Salwa al-Khammash, *Arab Women and the Traditional Backward Society* (Dar al-Hakika, Beirut, n.d. In Arabic), p.92.

7. Carla Makhlouf, *Changing Veils* (Croom Helm, London, 1979), p.68.

8. In Iraq schools and universities are mixed at all ages except 12 to 18, which is considered a dangerous time when the sexes should not mix.

9. For an investigation of Iraqi women's attitude to clothes, see Hala al-Badri, *Iraqi Women* (General Federation of Iraqi Women, Baghdad, 1980. In Arabic).

Chapter 1

1. Julian Pitt-Rivers, 'Honour and Social Status', in J.G. Peristiany (ed.), *Honour and Shame* (Weidenfeld & Nicolson, London, 1965).

2. Unni Wikan, 'Shame and Honour, A Contestable Pair', *Man*, vol. 19, no. 4 (1984), p.636.

3. R. Patai, *The Arab Mind* (Scribner's, New York, 1973).

4. Naila Minai, *Women in Islam* (John Murray, London, 1981), p.114.

5. 'Washing off the shame' was originally a bedouin custom.

6. Ann Oakley, in her book *Sex, Gender and Society* (Temple-Smith, London, 1976), notes similar attitudes in English society-even newborn babies receive a gender and infant boys are treated differently from infant girls.

7. Patai, *Arab Mind*, p.29.

8. A face like a moon means a beautiful face. See Salwa al-Khammash, *Arab Women and the Traditional Backward Society* (Dar al-Hakika, Beirut, n.d. In Arabic).

9. An Iraqi proverb runs, *walad majnoon wala binit katoon*, meaning, 'A crazy boy is preferable to a *katoon* girl.' *Katoon* describes the concept of the most perfect girl imaginable, one who possesses all the 'feminine' virtues and household skills as well as being beautiful and charming.

10. Even if a man does not have a son, he might expect to be called by a notional son's name. For example, a man called Muhammad might have the nickname of Abu Jassem (father of Jassem), even though he has no sons. His wife would be known as Um Jassem.

11. The girls' names Nihaya, Muntaha, Intihaa, Basaad, Khitaam, and so on, all mean 'end' or 'enough'. Girls are given these names in the superstitious belief that the mother will only bear male children after that.

12. Nawal El Saadawi, *The Hidden Face of Eve* (Zed Press, London, 1980), p.26.

13. Nazik al-Malaika, *A Tranquil Moment of a Wave* (n. pub., Beirut, 1957. In Arabic), p.146.

14. Nawal El Saadawi, *Woman and Sex*, vol. 1 (al-Muasasa al-Arabiyya lil-Dirasat wal-Nashr, Beirut, 1974. In Arabic), p.47.

15. For further information on this, see Elizabeth W. Fernea,

Guests of the Sheik (Robert Hale, London, 1965), p.238; and Halim Barakat, 'The Arab Family and the Challenge of Social Transformation' in E.W. Fernea (ed.), *Women and the Family in the Middle East, New Voices of Change* (University of Texas Press, Austin, 1985), pp.31–2.

16. See the women's comments on female bosses and why they preferred men in the Introduction and Conclusion.

17. As described by Sania Hamady in *Temperament and Character of the Arabs* (Twayne, New York, 1960), pp.44–8.

18. See also Patai, *Arab Mind*, pp.160–1; and Daisy Hilse Dwyer, *Images and Self-Images: Male and Female in Morocco* (Columbia University Press, New York, 1978), pp.111–12.

19. Alcoholism among men is examined in more detail in Chapter 4.

20. For example, there is a common saying: 'He who teaches you one letter owns you as a slave.' And a line of poetry states: 'Stand up and pay your respects to your teacher as he enters. A teacher is almost as holy as a prophet.'

Chapter 2

1. M. Kamel Nahas, 'The Family in the Arab World', *Marriage and Family Living*, vol. 16, no. 4 (1954), p.294.

2. Ihsan M. al-Hassan, 'Social Structure and Family Change in Iraq under Conditions of Industrialisation', unpublished PhD thesis, Hungarian Academy of Sciences, Budapest, 1977, p.69.

3. Janet Abu-Lughod and Lucy Amin observed a similar situation among Egyptian women. See 'Egyptian Marriage Advertisements: Microcosm of a Changing Society', *Marriage and Family Living*, vol. 23, no. 2 (1961), p.127.

4. Research suggests that such changes began to materialize in the early 1950s.

5. This view is supported by the sayings of Muhammad: 'Seek non-relations or else you will become weak' and 'Do not marry

relations, particularly close ones, as the offspring will be weak.'
Samya Hassan al-Saaty, *Marriage, Mate Selection and Social Change*
(Ain Shams, Cairo, 1972. In Arabic), p.104.

6. The same point was made by Nermin Abadan, 'Turkey', in
Raphael Patai (ed.), *Women in the Modern World* (Collier-
Macmillan, London, 1967), p.92. In a study carried out among
Turkish university students, Abadan found that the majority of
men would refuse to marry a girl who had been friendly with a
person of the opposite sex. In contrast, such social intercourse is
regarded as normal in most Western countries.

7. Ali al-Wardi, *Social Aspects of Modern Iraqi History*, part 1
(Irshad Press, Baghdad, 1969. In Arabic), pp.293–9.

8. See Sayed Owais, *Discussion on Contemporary Egyptian Women*
(Atlas, Cairo, 1977. In Arabic), p.193.

9. Hashem al-Mallah and Muhammad Dahish, *Love and Marriage
at the University* (General Federation of Iraqi Women, Baghdad,
n.d. In Arabic), p.6.

10. Nadia Youssef, 'Cultural Ideals, Feminine Behaviour and
Family Control', *Comparative Studies in Society and History*, vol. 15,
no. 3 (1973), p.334.

11. An Iraqi saying goes, *narak walla jannat hali*. It means, 'I
prefer your hell to my family's heaven' and is always quoted when
problems arise between husband and wife. For example, after
having a row with her husband, the wife might return to her
parents or to her brothers or sisters, but then have problems living
with them.

12. From her research on Egyptian society, al-Saaty has
observed similar types of change (al-Saaty, *Marriage*, p.385).

Chapter 3

1. Nawal El Saadawi, *The Hidden Face of Eve* (Zed Press,
London, 1980), p.26.

2. Ibid., p.44.

3. Similar observations have been made about Turkish women: 'the marriagable girl should be known as untouched by any hand . . . a man may claim that he was kept in ignorance of the fact that his wife was not a virgin and may be granted a divorce.' Fatma Mansur Cosar, 'Women in Turkish Society', in Lois Beck and Nikki Keddic (eds), *Women in the Muslim World* (Harvard University Press, Mass., 1980), p.126.

4. This situation is also found in Iran. Writing on Iranian women, Vieille notes: 'The woman, for her part, must not in any case show that she has a desire. Even in married life it would be improper; she must affect as much indifference toward sexuality as she showed disinterest in her own marriage . . . Only a man has the right to want to make love, . . . and only he is promised its enjoyment.' Paul Vieille, 'Iranian Women in Family Alliance and Sexual Politics', in Beck and Keddie (eds), *Women in the Muslim World*, pp.462–3.

5. For a similar observation, see Lee Rainwater, 'Marital Sexuality in Four Cultures of Poverty', *Marriage and the Family*, vol. 26, no. 4 (1964), p.458.

6. See Azzat Hijazi, 'Does the Arab Woman Play a Valuable Role in Development?', *Social Science Journal*, 1st part special issue, vol. 5 (1981). In Arabic; p.271.

7. For a similar observation, see Rainwater, 'Marital Sexuality', p.458.

8. See Fatima Mernissi, *Beyond the Veil: Male-Female Dynamics in a Modern Muslim Society* (John Wiley, New York, 1975), pp.106–7; and El Saadawi, *Hidden Face of Eve*, p.149.

9. R. Patai, *The Arab Mind* (Scribner's, New York, 1973), p.33.

10. El Saadawi, *Hidden Face of Eve*, pp.74–5.

Chapter 4

1. Elizabeth W. Fernea, *Guests of the Sheik* (Robert Hale, London, 1965), pp.237–8.

2. This was discussed earlier in Chapter 1.

3. This situation is neatly summed up in an Iraqi proverb, *al-nassib, thib*, meaning, 'The son-in-law is a wolf' [so be careful in dealing with him].

4. See also Hanna Papanek, 'Purdah: Separate Worlds and Symbolic Shelter', *International Quarterly*, vol. 5, no. 35 (1973), p.301.

5. See for example, Raja Muhammad Qasim, 'The Working Woman in Iraq: a Social-Demographic Study of the Woman Worker's Role in Iraq', unpublished MA thesis, College of Arts, Baghdad University, 1984 (in Arabic).

6. See Dorothy Smith, 'An Analysis of Ideological Structures and How Women are Excluded', *Canadian Review of Sociology and Anthropology*, vol. 12, no. 4 (1975), p.354; and Daisy Hilse Dwyer, *Images and Self-Images: Male and Female in Morocco* (Columbia University Press, New York, 1978), p.16.

7. Naila Minai, *Women in Islam* (John Murray, London, 1981), p.182.

8. An Iraqi proverb goes, *kulshi din hata dmoa al-ain*, meaning, 'Everything in life is debt, even tears.' In other words, if someone cries for my dead, I am expected to cry for theirs.

Chapter 5

1. In Iraq it is customary to slaughter a sheep as a means of celebration. The meat is then cut up and should be given to the needy. This is a religious practice, meant to act as a thanksgiving.

2. After completing their training, teachers are required by law to work in a village or small town. After a few years, those from the cities are transferred back home. This is meant to ensure a uniform standard of education throughout Iraq.

3. Nawal El Saadawi, *Woman and Neurosis* (al-Muasasa al-Arabiyya lil-Dirasat wal-Nashr, Beirut, 1977. In Arabic), pp.105–6.

Chapter 6

1. See Hamed Ammar, *Growing Up in an Egyptian Village* (Routledge & Kegan Paul, London, 1954), p.115.

2. Elizabeth W. Fernea, *Guests of the Sheik* (Robert Hale, London, 1965), p.83.

3. Research from India has revealed a similar situation, when the husband seeks the help of neighbours or relatives. See Ursula Sharma, *Women, Work and Property in North-West India* (Tavistock, London, 1980), p.93.

4. Working women spend their earnings in many ways. Some spend it on themselves, the children and the household. Others save or invest it, depending on the husband's income. It is unlikely that the wife would be forced to share her income if the husband was earning a high salary, as this would go against the Arab image of manhood.

5. Ann Oakley, *The Sociology of Housework* (Martin Robertson, Oxford, 1978), p.104.

6. Afifa El-Bustani, 'Problems Facing a Selected Group of Iraqi Women', unpublished PhD thesis, Teachers College, Columbia University, New York, 1956, pp.59–61.

Chapter 7

1. Janet Abu-Lughod and Lucy Amin, 'Egyptian Marriage Advertisements: Microcosm of a Changing Society', *Marriage and Family Living*, vol. 23, no. 2 (1961), p.130.

2. Zahra's marriage was conducted at home by a *sayyid* (religious official) and was not officially registered with the courts due to her age.

3. Nawal El Saadawi, *The Hidden Face of Eve* (Zed Press, London, 1980), p.55.

4. Naila Minai, *Women in Islam* (John Murray, London, 1981), p.144.

5. Afifa El-Bustani, 'Problems Facing a Selected Group of

Iraqi Women', unpublished PhD thesis, Teachers College, Columbia University, New York, 1956), p.111.

6. Corruption (*tahalol*) and freedom (*taharror*).

7. The General Federation of Iraqi Women (GFIW) is a women's organization set up by the Iraqi government.

Conclusion

1. The case of Indian women after the menopause is very similar in that they under-emphasize their sexuality and dress in very simple clothes. See P. Jeffery, *Frogs in a Well* (Zed Press, London, 1979), p.107.

2. Shulamith Firestone, *The Dialectic of Sex* (Paladin, London, 1972).

3. Fatima Mernissi, *Beyond the Veil: Male-Female Dynamics in a Modern Muslim Society* (John Wiley, New York, 1975), p.xvi.

4. Ursula Sharma, 'Women and their Affines: The Veil as a Symbol of Separation', *Man*, vol. 13, no. 5 (1978), p.280.

5. See also Azizah al-Hibri, 'Capitalism is not an Advanced Stage of Patriarchy: But Marxism is not Feminism', in Lydia Sargeant (ed.), *The Unhappy Marriage of Marxism and Feminism* (Pluto, London, 1981), p.185; and Cynthia Nelson and Virginia Olesen, 'Veil of Illusion: a Critique of the Concept of Equality in Western Feminist Thought', *Catalyst*, vol. 10–11 (1972), p.29.

6. In Iraq old women traditionally say in their prayers, *rabi la hakim wala hakeem*, meaning 'May God preserve us from judges and doctors.'

7. Al-Hibri, 'Capitalism is not an Advanced Stage of Patriarchy'.

8. Ann Oakley, *The Sociology of Housework* (Martin Robertson, Oxford, 1978).

9. Lois Beck and Nikki Keddie (eds), *Women in the Muslim World* (Harvard University Press, Mass., 1980), p.19.

10. A similar observation has been made about Pakistani

society. See Hanna Papaek, 'Purdah: Separate Worlds and Symbolic Shelter', *International Quarterly*, vol. 5, no. 35 (1973), p.301.

11. An important reason for girls' education in Muslim societies is that it reflects the personal status of the men in the family. See Alya Baffoun, 'Women and Social Change in the Muslim Arab World', *Women's Studies International Forum*, vol. 5, no. 2 (1982), p.232.

12. Naila Minai, *Women in Islam* (John Murray, London, 1981).

13. A similar finding to mine has been noted in Pakistan. See Papanek, 'Purdah', p.299.

14. Nelson and Olesen, 'Veil of Illusion', pp.74–5.

15. Ursula Sharma, 'Are Women Committed to Paid Work? Some Data from Simla, North India', in Barbara D. Miller and Janice Hyde (eds), *Women in Asia and Asian Studies* (Syracuse University, New York, 1984), p.38.

16. See Minai, *Women in Islam*, pp.206–9.

17. Simone de Beauvoir, *The Second Sex* (Penguin, Harmondsworth, 1979), p.710.

18. Daisy Hilse Dwyer ('Women's Conflict Behaviour in a Traditional Moroccan Setting: An Interactional Analysis', unpublished PhD thesis, Yale University, 1973, p.28) and Nawal El Saadawi (*Woman and Sex*, vol. 2, al-Muasasa al-Arabiyya lil-Dirasat wal-Nashr, Beirut, 1974. In Arabic) found the same thing in Morocco and Egypt respectively.

19. Pauline Hunt, *Gender and Class Consciousness* (Macmillan, London, 1980).

20. Raja Muhammad Qasim, 'The Working Woman in Iraq: a Social-Demographic Study of the Woman Worker's Role in Iraq', unpublished MA thesis, Baghdad University, 1984.

21. Work on French wives has made the same point. See Christine Delphy, *The Main Enemy: A Materialist Analysis of Women's Oppression* (Women's Research and Resources Centre Publication, no. 3, 1977).

22. Ibid.

Select Bibliography

Abadan, Nermin, 'Turkey', in Raphael Patai (ed.), *Women in the Modern World*, Collier-Macmillan, London, 1967.

Abou-Zeid, Ahmed, 'Honour and Shame Among the Bedouins of Egypt', in J.G. Peristiany (ed.), *Honour and Shame*, Weidenfeld & Nicolson, London, 1965.

Abu-Lughod, Janet and Lucy Amin, 'Egyptian Marriage Advertisements: Microcosm of a Changing Society', *Marriage and Family Living*, vol. 23, no. 2, 1961: 127–36.

al-Badri, Hala, *Iraqi Women (al-Mara al-Iraqiyya)*, General Federation of Iraqi Women, Baghdad, 1980 (Arabic).

al-Hassan, Ihsan M., 'Social Structure and Family Change in Iraq under Conditions of Industrialisation', unpublished PhD thesis, Hungarian Academy of Sciences, Budapest, 1977.

_____ *The Effects of Industrialization on the Social Status of Iraqi Women*, General Federation of Iraqi Women, Baghdad, 1980 (Arabic).

al-Hibri, Azizah, 'Capitalism is not an Advanced Stage of Patriarchy: But Marxism is not Feminism', in Lydia Sargeant (ed.), *The Unhappy Marriage of Marxism and Feminism*, Pluto, London, 1981.

_____ Editorial, *Women's Studies International Forum*, vol. 5, no. 2, 1982: v–viii.

_____ 'A Study of Islamic Herstory: or how did we ever get into this mess?' *Women's Studies International Forum*, vol. 5, no. 2, 1982: 207–19.

al-Khammash, Salwa, *Arab Women and the Traditional Backward Society* (*al-Mara al-Arabiyya wal-Mujtama al-Taklidi al-Mutakhallif*), Dar al-Hakika, Beirut, n.d. (Arabic).

al-Malaika, Nazik, *A Tranquil Moment of a Wave*, n. pub., Beirut, 1957 (Arabic).

al-Mallah, Hashem and Muhammad Dahish, *Love and Marriage at the University* (*al-Hub wal-Zawaj fi al-Jamiaa*), General Federation of Iraqi Women, Baghdad, n.d. (Arabic).

al-Saaty, Samya Hassan, *Marriage, Mate Selection and Social Change* (*al-Ikhtiyar lil-Zawage wal-Takaun al-Ijtimai*), Ain Shams, Cairo, 1972 (Arabic).

al-Wardi, Ali, *A Study of Iraqi Society* (*Dirasa fi al-Mujtama al-Iraqi*), Irshad Press, Baghdad, 1965 (Arabic).

_____ *Social Aspects of Modern Iraqi History* (*Lamahat min Tarikh al-Iraq al-Hadith*), part 1, Irshad Press, Baghdad, 1969 (Arabic).

Ammar, Hamed, *Growing up in an Egyptian Village*, Routledge & Kegan Paul, London, 1954.

Antoun, Richard T., 'On the Modesty of Women in Arab Muslim Villages', *American Anthropologist*, vol. 70, 1968: 671–97.

Baffoun, Alya, 'Women and Social Change in the Muslim Arab World', *Women's Studies International Forum*, vol. 5, no. 2, 1982: 227–42.

Barakat, Halim, 'The Arab Family and the Challenge of Social Transformation', in E.W. Fernea (ed.), *Women and the Family in the Middle East, New Voices of Change*, University of Texas Press, Austin, 1985.

Beck, Lois and Nikki Keddie, 'Introduction', in Lois Beck and Nikki Keddie (eds), *Women in the Muslim World*, Harvard University Press, Mass., 1980.

Beechy, Veronica, 'On Patriarchy', *Feminist Review*, no. 3, 1979: 66: 82.

Belotti, Elena Gianini, *Little Girls*, Writers & Readers Publishing Co-operative, London, 1975.

Berger, Morroe, *The Arab World Today*, Doubleday, New York, 1964.

Camilleri, Carmel, 'Modernity and the Family in Tunisia', *Journal of Marriage and the Family*, vol. 29, 1967: 590–95.

Campbell, J.K., 'Honour and the Devil', in J.G. Peristiany, (ed.), *Honour and Shame*, Weidenfeld & Nicolson, London, 1965.

Cosar, Fatma Mansur, 'Women in Turkish Society', in Lois Beck and Nikki Keddie (eds), *Women in the Muslim World*, Harvard University Press, Mass., 1980.

Coulson, Margaret, Branka Magas and Hilary Wainwright, 'The Housewife and her Labour under Capitalism – a Critique', in Ellen Malos (ed.), *The Politics of Housework*, Allison & Busby, London, 1980.

de Beauvoir, Simone, *The Second Sex*, Penguin, Harmondsworth, 1979.

Dehyab, Fawzia, *Social Values and Habits (al-Keiam wal-Adat al-Ijtimaia)*, Dar al-Kitab al-Arabi lil-Tibaa wal-Nashr, Cairo, 1966 (Arabic).

Delphy, Christine, *The Main Enemy: A Materialist Analysis of Women's Oppression*, Women's Research and Resources Centre Publication, Exploration in Feminism, no. 3, 1977.

Dwyer, Daisy Hilse, 'Women's Conflict Behaviour in a Traditional Moroccan Setting: An Interactional Analysis', unpublished PhD thesis, Yale University, 1973.

——————— *Images and Self-Images: Male and Female in Morocco*, Columbia University Press, New York, 1978.

Eisenstein, Hester, *Contemporary Feminist Thought*, Unwin, London, 1984.

Eisenstein, Zillah, 'Developing a Theory of Capitalist Patriarchy and Socialist Feminism', in Zillah Eisenstein (ed.), *Capitalist Patriarchy and the Case of Socialist Feminists*, Monthly Review Press, New York, 1979.

_____ 'Reform and/or Revolution: Toward a United Women's Movement', in Lydia Sargeant (ed.), *The Unhappy Marriage of Marxism and Feminism*, Pluto, London, 1981.

El-Bustani, Afifa, 'Problems Facing a Selected Group of Iraqi Women', unpublished PhD thesis, Teachers College, Columbia University, New York, 1956.

El Saadawi, Nawal, *Woman and Sex (al-Mara wal-Jins)*, vols. 1 & 2, al-Muasasa al-Arabiyya lil-Dirasat wal-Nashr, Beirut, 1974 (Arabic).

_____ *Woman and Neurosis (al-Mara wal-Sira al-Nafsi)*, al-Muasasa al-Arabiyya lil-Dirasat wal-Nashr, Beirut, 1977 (Arabic).

_____ *The Hidden Face of Eve*, Zed Press, London, 1980.

Fernea, Elizabeth W., *Guests of the Sheik*, Robert Hale, London, 1965.

_____ and Basima Quattan Bezirgan, 'Introduction', in Elizabeth W. Fernea and Basima Quattan Bezirgan (eds), *Middle Eastern Muslim Women Speak*, University of Texas Press, Austin, 1980.

_____ 'Introduction', in Elizabeth W. Fernea (ed.), *Women and the Family in the Middle East, New Voices of Change*, University of Texas Press, Austin, 1985.

Figes, Eva, *Patriarchal Attitudes, Women in Society*, Faber, London, 1970.

Firestone, Shulamith, *The Dialectic of Sex*, Paladin, London, 1972.

Friedman, Scarlet, 'The Marxist Paradigm: Radical Feminist Theorists Compared', *British Sociological Association*, 1982 Conference — Gender and Society.

Gardiner, Jean, Susan Himmelweit and Maureen Mackintosh,

'Women's Domestic Labour', in Ellen Malos (ed.), *The Politics of Housework*, Allison & Busby, London, 1980.

Hamady, Sania, *Temperament and Character of the Arabs*, Twayne, New York, 1960.

Hijazi, Azzat, 'Does the Arab Woman Play a Valuable Role in Development?' (*al-Mara al-Arabiyya hal Toadi Dawran tho Kima fi al-Tanmya?*), *Social Science Journal*, 1st part special issue, vol. 5, 1981 (Arabic).

Hunt, Pauline, *Gender and Class Consciousness*, Macmillan, London, 1980.

Jeffery, Patricia, *Frogs in a Well: Indian Women in Purdah*, Zed Press, London, 1979.

Joseph, Suad, 'The Mobilization of Iraqi Women into the Wage Labour Force', *Women and Politics in Twentieth Century Africa and Asia, Studies in Third World Societies*, no. 16, 1982: 69–90.

Keddie, Nikki, 'Problems in the Study of Middle Eastern Women', *International Journal of Middle East Studies*, vol. 10, 1979: 225–40.

Makhlouf, Carla, *Changing Veils*, Croom Helm, London, 1979.

Mernissi, Fatima, *Beyond the Veil: Male-Female Dynamics in a Modern Muslim Society*, John Wiley, New York, 1975.

_____ 'Virginity and Patriarchy', *Women's Studies International Forum*, vol. 5, no. 2, 1982: 183–91.

Minai, Naila, *Women in Islam*, John Murray, London, 1981.

Mohsen, Safia, 'New Images, Old Reflections: Working Middle-Class Women in Egypt', in Elizabeth W. Fernea (ed.), *Women and the Family in the Middle East, New Voices of Change*, University of Texas Press, Austin, 1985.

Molyneux, Maxine, 'Women in Socialist Societies', in Kate Young, Carol Wolkowitz & Roslyn McCullagh (eds), *Of Marriage and the Market: Women's Subordination Internationally and Its Lessons*, Routledge, London 1981.

Nahas, M. Kamel, 'The Family in the Arab World', *Marriage and Family Living*, vol. 16, no. 4, 1954: 293–300.

Nelson, Cynthia, 'Changing Roles of Men and Women', *Anthropological Quarterly*, vol. 4, no. 2, 1968: 57–77.

——————— and Virginia Olesen, 'Veil of Illusion: a Critique of the Concept of Equality in Western Feminist Thought', *Catalyst*, vol. 10–11, 1972: 8–37.

——————— 'Public and Private, Politics: Women in the Middle East World', *American Ethnologist*, vol. 1, part 3, 1974: 551–63.

Oakley, Ann, *Sex, Gender and Society*, Temple-Smith, London, 1976.

——————— *Housewife*, Pelican, Harmondsworth, 1977.

——————— *The Sociology of Housework*, Martin Robertson, Oxford, 1978.

——————— 'Interviewing Women: a Contradiction in Terms', in Helen Roberts (ed.), *Doing Feminist Research*, Routledge & Kegan Paul, London, 1981.

——————— *The Subject Women*, Fontana, London, 1982.

Omvedt, Gail, *We Will Smash This Prison: Indian Women in Struggle*, Zed Press, London, 1980.

Owais, Sayed, *Discussion on Contemporary Egyptian Women (Hadith an al-Mara al-Masriyya al-Moasira)*, National Centre for Social and Criminological Research, Atlas, Cairo, 1977 (Arabic).

Papanek, Hanna, 'Purdah: Separate Worlds and Symbolic Shelter', *International Quarterly*, vol. 5, no. 35, 1973: 289–325.

Pastner, Carroll, McC., 'A Social, Structural and Historical Analysis of Honour, Shame and Purdah', *Anthropological Quarterly*, vol. 45, no. 4, Catholic University of America Press, Washington, D.C., 1972: 248–59.

Patai, R., *Golden River to Golden Road*, University of Pennsylvania Press, 1967.

——————— *The Arab Mind*, Scribner's, New York, 1973.

Peristiany, J.G., 'Introduction', in J.G. Peristiany (ed.), *Honour and Shame*, Weidenfeld & Nicolson, London, 1965.

Pitt-Rivers, Julian, 'Honour and Social Status', in J.G. Peristiany (ed.), *Honour and Shame*, Weidenfeld & Nicolson, London, 1965.

Qasim, Raja Muhammad, 'The Working Woman in Iraq: a Social-Demographic Study of the Woman Worker's Role in Iraq' (*al-Mara al-Amila fi al-Iraq: Dirasa Ijtimaia Dimographia li-Dawr al-Mara al-Amila fi al-Iraq*), unpublished MA thesis, College of Arts, Baghdad University, 1984.

Rainwater, Lee, 'Marital Sexuality in Four Cultures of Poverty', *Marriage and the Family*, vol. 26, no. 4, 1964: 457–65.

Randall, Vicky, *Women and Politics*, Macmillan, London, 1982.

Rowbotham, Sheila, 'The Trouble With Patriarchy', in Mary Evans (ed.), *The Woman Question*, Fontana, London, 1982.

_____ *Woman's Consciousness, Man's World*, Penguin, Harmondsworth, 1983.

Shalash, Amal, 'Development of Iraq 1950–1980 with Reference to Changes in the Labour Force in a Planned Economy', unpublished PhD thesis, University of Salford, 1983.

Sharma, Ursula, 'Segregation and its Consequences in India', in Patricia Caplan and Janet M. Bujra (eds), *Women United Women Divided*, Tavistock, London, 1978.

_____ 'Women and their Affines: The Veil as a Symbol of Separation', *Man*, vol. 13, no. 5, 1978: 218–33.

_____ *Women, Work and Property in North-West India*, Tavistock, London, 1980.

_____ 'Are Women Committed to Paid Work? Some Data from Simla, North India', in Barbara D. Miller and Janice Hyde (eds), *Women in Asia and Asian Studies*, CWAS, Monography Series, no. 1, Committee on Women in Asian Studies, Syracuse University, New York, 1984.

Smith, Dorothy, 'An Analysis of Ideological Structures and How

Women are Excluded', *Canadian Review of Sociology and Anthropology*, vol. 12, no. 4, 1975: 352–39.

Spender, Dale, *Man Made Language*, Routledge & Kegan Paul, London, 1980.

Stacey, Judith, 'When Patriarchy Kowtows', in Zillah Eisenstein (ed.), *Capitalist Patriarchy and the Case of Socialist Feminists*, *Monthly Review Press*, New York, 1979.

Standing, Hilary, with Bela Bandyopadhyaya, 'Women's Employment and the Household; some findings from Calcutta', *Economic and Political Weekly*, vol. 20, no. 17, Review of Women's Studies, 1985: 1–17.

Tapper, Nancy, 'Mysteries of the Harem? An Anthropological Perspective on Recent Studies of Women of the Muslim Middle East', *Women's Studies International Quarterly*, vol. 2, no. 4, 1979: 481–7.

Van Dusen, Roxanna, 'The Study of Women in the Middle East: Some Thoughts', *Middle East Studies Association Bulletin*, vol. 10, part 2, 1976: 1–19.

Vieille, Paul, 'Iranian Women in Family Alliance and Sexual Politics', in Lois Beck and Nikki Keddie (eds), *Women in the Muslim World*, Harvard University Press, Mass., 1980.

Wikan, Unni, 'Man Becomes Woman', *Man*, vol. 12, 1977: 304–19.

_____ *Life Among the Poor in Cairo*, Tavistock, London, 1980.

_____ 'Shame and Honour, A Contestable Pair', *Man*, vol. 19, no. 4, 1984: 635–51.

Youssef, Nadia, 'Cultural Ideals, Feminine Behaviour and Family Control', *Comparative Studies in Society and History*, vol. 15, no. 3, 1973: 326–47.